CANNABIS COOKBOOK:

How to extract and make your own CBD & THC for Medical Marijuana Recipes. start cooking Pizza, DESSERTS, SAVORY MEALS and more

Introduction 3

Chapter 1. : Cannabis Plant Basics 4

Chapter 2. : Medical Uses Of Cannabis 11

Chapter 3. : What Are Thc And Cbd? 14

Chapter 4. : All About Decarboxylating 17

Chapter 5. How To Extract Thc 19

Chapter 6. : Complete Extraction Methods 23

Chapter 7. : Guide On How To Calculate Thc Dose For Recipes 27

Chapter 8. : Tips And Tricks For Cooking With Cannabis 30

Chapter 9. : Infusing Oils And Butter 32

Chapter 10. : Appetizer Recipes 37

Chapter 11. : Savory Meals 48

Chapter 12. : Cookies 61

Chapter 13. : Bars And Brownies 72

Chapter 14. : Cakes 81

Chapter 15. : Drinks 92

Conclusion 98

Introduction

You have likely come across the word cannabis, weed, marijuana, or other terms in your life and wondered what it stands for. Well, let us find out! Cannabis is an herb that is extensively grown in most Asian and African countries. The grass is used in making traditional medicines and also smoked to avail of its therapeutic effects. Cannabis contains a chemical known as THC, which is chiefly responsible for inducing psychoactive effects on the mind. Smoking it, by wrapping the dried leaves in a joint, is sure to send you on a mental trip. It is quite popular among youngsters and older people around the world and considered to be one of the most potent and safe, psychoactive herbs in the world.

There are many ways in how marijuana can be induced and applied, either by smoking, vaping, as topical, and growing popularly now is through ingesting it. Yes, that's right; many people are aware of the fact that the herb can be used in cooking, as well. Cannabis can serve as a cooking ingredient and a very trippy one at that! Because of its distinct flavor and aroma, cannabis is extensively used in the preparation of food, which not only satisfies hunger but also gives you a nice high. If you have ever smoked up, then you will know how it can transport you mentally into a state of relaxation, and you can expect the same from the prepared dishes.

Whether you are interested in cannabis-infused edibles for medical reasons, recreational ones, or just for the novelty, it is a pretty fun activity that brings together art and science. A love of baking and cooking is all you need to get started. We've compiled and distilled our expertise in all things edibles into this guide to get you started with creating your homemade edibles safely and effectively. The beauty of homemade edibles lies in the ability to control and personalize your creations—whether you are nut-free, gluten-free, vegan, or Paleo. And making your infusions allows you to manage your potency and build confidence in knowing what the effects will be.

This book will serve as your one true cannabis guide and give you recipes that you can try out at home. It will also give you sufficient information on the plant so that you can cook with ease.

The recipes for cannabis edibles given in this book are quite easy to understand and simple to follow. Well, cooking with cannabis isn't that complicated, is it? All that you need to do is gather the right ingredients and follow the recipes given in this book. Make sure that you are cautious while cooking with cannabis. Also, it is always a good idea to consult a medical practitioner before you start consuming any cannabis-infused products. Another thing that you cannot afford to ignore is verifying whether using cannabis is legal in your area or not! So, let us get started without any further ado!

Chapter 1. : Cannabis Plant Basics

The Cannabis Plant

Let's start with a primer on cannabis terminology and anatomy. Working your way up from the soil, beginning with the stem of the plant, you'll start to see fan leaves (the iconic marijuana leaf) up until the primary bud, or cola. This is the flower. Smaller buds grow from the nodes between fan leaves. The buds are made up of calyxes, which contain the highest concentration of trichomes, or plant resin. Extending past the calyxes are tiny orange hairs—the pistils. All you need to know about pistils is that they play an essential role in the plant's reproduction.

The flower/bud is what people smoke. Though iconic, the fan leaves of the plant are the least potent and usually just tossed out at harvest. Smaller leaves that are close to the buds are sugar leaves or trim leaves. These are great to use in infusions/extracts. Just like the flowers, they are coated in trichomes. The stem is very low in potency but is thought to have a decent concentration of CBD.

If you walked into a cannabis dispensary today, chances are you'd be presented with three or more categories of cannabis flower: Sativa, Indica, and hybrids, which may be further categorized into Sativa-dominant hybrid, an Indica-dominant hybrid, or split hybrids. However, the distinction of Sativa versus Indica is quickly losing its importance. When researchers analyzed nearly 500 strains, they found no

evidence that the "indicas" were chemically distinct from the "Sativas." The emerging opinion today is that the range of effects produced from different cannabis strains comes down to the ratio of cannabinoids and terpenes, the chemical compounds found in the plant's resin. It will be interesting to see how the categorization of the strains develops.

Sativa

Sativa strains tend to yield tall plants that are high in THC and have long, finger-like leaves. They are known for giving stimulating, creative "head" highs filled with laughter and in-depth conversations. On the flip side, they have also been known to increase feelings of anxiety and paranoia. Some Sativa strains are thought to enhance lights and sounds, making them great for enjoying music, movies, or the outdoors. Popular Sativa includes Sour Diesel, Green Crack, Jack Herer, Durban Poison, and Lemon Haze.

Indica

Indica strains are shorter, stockier, and have broad leaves. They tend to flower faster than Sativas and produce a higher yield. Indicas are known for providing a more relaxing, full-body experience that's ideal for the treatment of pain, muscle spasms, anxiety, nausea, loss of appetite, and sleep. Some effects have been described as "couch lock," which can be good or bad depending on how you see it. Famous Indicas include Bubba Kush, Northern Lights, Purple Kush, Blueberry, and G13.

Hybrids

Each season, growers develop new hybrids by crossbreeding select strains to produce a whole new variety tailored to meet desired effects. Hybrids cover a vast area in the crossbreeding of Sativas and Indicas, creating specialty strains that are bred for specific traits from each species. Many of the most-loved strains are hybrids, like Blue Dream, Girl Scout Cookies (GSC), OG Kush, Pineapple Express, and Trainwreck.

Cannabinoids

The plant's resin contains hundreds of chemical compounds in the form of cannabinoids and terpenes. When the cannabinoids enter the bloodstream, they activate cannabinoid receptors throughout the endocannabinoid system in our bodies, producing a range of effects. Cannabinoid receptors are found throughout the human body: They are in the brain, organs, central and peripheral nervous system, cardiovascular system, reproductive system, gastrointestinal system, urinary system, immune system, and even cartilage. The endocannabinoid system regulates the homeostasis of our biological functions — appetite, memory, metabolism, female reproduction, sleep, immune response, thermoregulation, pain, autonomic nervous system, and stress response — and is considered the most crucial system in the human body.

Let's say that one more time—it is considered the most crucial system in the human body. Our bodies naturally make endocannabinoids to stimulate the cannabinoid receptors and regulate the system. Cannabinoids such as THC and CBD are external substances that stimulate these same receptors. This certainly explains how cannabis can provide such a range of benefits across a vast array of conditions and illnesses. Research indicates that the introduction of external cannabinoids like THC can cause the endocannabinoid system to create more receptors and increase an individual's future sensitivity to the cannabinoids.

Conversely, the endocannabinoid system has also been shown to restrict the number of receptors when it experiences an overabundance of cannabinoids.

An interesting side note here: Research shows that taking a break from cannabis for 28 days (also known as a tolerance break) can reset the body's endocannabinoid system to its pre-cannabis state. This self-regulation makes sense for a system known to control the body's homeostasis.

THC/THCA

THC, tetrahydrocannabinol, is the most well-known cannabinoid, and appropriately so, in our opinion. It is not only responsible for the beloved psychoactive effects but also for relieving pain, nausea, lack of appetite, and inflammation. THC mimics the cannabinoids naturally produced in the body and activates receptors in the brain associated with thinking, pain, pleasure, time perception, coordination, and concentration. It sticks to receptors of cannabinoid of the immune and nervous system, which yields to a person feeling is relaxed, lesser pain, and an increase in food intake, which is responsible for giving us a case of the "munchies." THC also appears to protect the brain by reducing inflammation and stimulating neurogenesis.

In raw cannabis, you will find THCA instead of THC. Once heated (decarboxylated), THCA becomes THC. THCA is not psychoactive and brings its own set of medicinal benefits. It has antiproliferative and anti-inflammatory abilities and helps in treating disorders of the immune system THCA has been used to treat cancer, muscle spasms, seizures, lupus, arthritis, endometriosis, and menstrual cramps. Raw plants can be juiced for THCA. Non-heated tinctures can also be made with high levels of THCA.

CBD/CBDA
Quickly gaining popularity is the now federally legal cannabidiol, CBD. It seems like you can't walk two blocks without seeing a sign for it these days. CBD is the second most prevalent cannabinoid and acts on different receptors throughout the body than THC, so there are little, if any, psychotropic results. Studies have shown that CBD offers pain relief and has anti-inflammatory and anti-anxiety properties. Research is now focusing on CBD in its treatment of epilepsy, Crohn's disease, PTSD, and multiple sclerosis, just to name a few. CBD has also been shown to reduce the effects of THC, which in large quantities, can be very unpleasant. Like THC, CBD starts as a different cannabinoid, CBDA, and must be heated (decarboxylated) to convert it into CBD. CBDA may be helpful as an anti-convulsant and to relieve nausea, pain, and inflammation. It may even have cancer-preventing properties. CBDA can be obtained through raw CBD-dominant strains.
CBG

Cannabigerol (CBG) is also growing in importance. CBG is non-psychoactive and responsible for the production of both THC and CBD. Plants that are harvested three-quarters of the way through the flowering cycle may preserve some CBG. A strain that is high in CBG (around 1 percent) is Harlequin. CBG has sedating, antimicrobial, antioxidant, and anti-inflammatory properties and can treat IBS, glaucoma (by lowering intraocular pressure), and insomnia. Some studies show how it can eliminate cancer cells and inhibit tumor growth.

CBN
CBN is made when the THC is under oxygen and light. It can cause an intense body high and make consumers dizzy or tired. It has mild effects, and it makes the THC effects higher. Its medicinal effects include reducing epilepsy and muscle spasms, relieving intraocular pressure, and reducing depression. All strains can produce CBN when exposed to light and oxygen. It may also be possible to find CBN-rich products at your local dispensary.

Terpenes

You may notice distinct aromas across various strains of cannabis. The complex flavor profiles and signature smells of different cannabis strains come from their terpenes. Like cannabinoids, terpenes are excreted in the trichome resin and contribute to the overall effects of the plant. But unlike cannabinoids, terpenes are not only in cannabis — they are present in many of our everyday foods, flowers, and herbs, like lemon, mint, lavender, and berries. They are what give cannabis strains their unique aromas and flavors and may tell you more about a particular strain's effects than the name or categorization. Pinene smells of, well, pine, and promotes alertness. Myrcene, found in mango and thyme, smells earthy and tropical and is very sedating. Limonene is citrusy and a mood elevator.

During the decarboxylation, infusion, and cooking process, many terpenes are lost, but if you infuse low and slow, you can retain a decent amount of the plant's terpene profile. If you understand the flavor of your cannabis, you can know how to best pair it with your food. Smell your marijuana and let the taste linger. Understanding the aroma and taste of terpenes can make you a true "connoisseur."

CARYOPHYLLENE

Caryophyllene has been described as a terpene that acts as a cannabinoid. It turns out Caryophyllene interacts with the endocannabinoid system on the same receptor as CBD.

- Flavors/Aromas: Rich, peppery, spicy, woody

- Found in/Pairs well with Thai basil, cloves, black pepper, caraway, oregano, lavender, rosemary, cinnamon, hops

- Strains: Hash Plant, Super Silver Haze, Candyland, Death Star, Girl Scout Cookies (GSC)

Effects/Uses: Antiseptic, antibacterial, antifungal, anti-inflammatory; good for arthritis, ulcers, autoimmune disorders, and other gastrointestinal complications.

HUMULENE

Did you know that cannabis and hops are closely related? Humulene is the terpene responsible for giving both a similar aromatic, hoppy profile.

- Flavors/Aromas: Hops, earthy, musky, spicy

- Found in/Pairs well with basil, sage, clove, ginger, ginseng

- Strains: ACDC, Banana Kush, Durban Poison, OG Kush, Trainwreck

- Effects/Uses: Antibacterial, anti-inflammatory, antifungal, analgesic

IMONENE

Next to Myrcene, limonene is the most abundant terpene in cannabis and leads the "entourage" by increasing the absorption of other terpenes.

- Flavors/Aromas: Bright, citrusy

- Found in/Pairs well with Citrus rind, rosemary, juniper, peppermint

- Strains: OG Kush, Super Lemon Haze, Lemon Skunk

- Effects/Uses: Stress relief, good mood, antibacterial, antifungal, fights gastrointestinal problems, anxiety, and depression.

INALOOL

Once you start looking, you'll notice that linalool is frequently used for its scent in many skincare products. Linalool is naturally occurring in flowers and spices like basil and lavender.

- Flavor/Aroma: Floral, citrus notes, sweet, candy-like
- Found in/Pairs well with lavender, citrus, rosewood, coriander, mint, cinnamon, coriander, basil
- Strains: G13, LA Confidential, Lavender
- Effects/Uses: Antipsychotic, anti-epileptic, anti-anxiety, anti-acne, sedative, pain relief, antidepressant

MYRCENE

Myrcene, the most abundant terpene in cannabis, is perhaps also the essential terpene—its presence is said to determine if a strain is Indica or Sativa. Plants with 0.5 percent or more Myrcene are said to be Indica, and less than 0.5 percent are said to be Sativa. The sedating, relaxing effects of Myrcene play a significant role in the experience of a strain.

- Flavor/Aroma: Musky, earthy, herbal with notes of citrus and tropical fruit
- Found in/Pairs well with mango, hops, bay leaves, lemongrass, eucalyptus, thyme, basil
- Strains: White Widow, Harlequin, Pure Kush, Skunk #1

- Effects/Uses: Sedating, relaxing, pain relief, anti-spasm, anti-inflammatory, anti-insomnia, antibiotic

NEROLIDOL

This terpene improves transdermal absorption, making it a great additive to Topicals.

- Flavors/Aromas: Woody, fresh bark, floral

- Found in/Pairs well with ginger, lavender, lemongrass, jasmine, orange, tea tree

- Strains: Jack Herer, Skywalker OG, Sour Diesel, Island Sweet Skunk, Girl Scout Cookies (GSC), Blue Dream

- Effects/Uses: Antioxidant, antifungal, anticancer, antimicrobial, sedative

PINENE

This piney terpene is pretty natural to identify. And with its ability to improve short-term memory, you'll be able to remember you identified it!

- Flavors/Aromas: Sweet, pine

- Found in/Pairs well with pine, rosemary, basil, parsley, dill, orange

- Strains: Jack Herer, Chemdawg, Bubba Kush, Trainwreck, Super Silver Haze

- Effects/Uses: Asthma relief, anti-inflammatory, alertness, memory retention, may counteract THC effects

TERPINOLENE

Like linalool, Terpinolene is frequently used in fragranced items due to its pleasing smell.

- Flavors/Aromas: Woody, smoky, fresh, piney, herbal, floral

- Found in/Pairs well with Apples, cumin, tea tree, nutmeg

- Strains: Mostly exclusive to Sativas like Super Lemon Haze, Jack Herer

- Effects/Uses: Antifungal, antibacterial, anti-insomnia, antioxidant, anticarcinogenic, sedative

Chapter 2. : Medical Uses Of Cannabis

Stress and Anxiety
Cannabis oil is, therefore, worth exploring and studying further as it can relax our mind and activate our happy hormones in the bodies of those that use it. This combination of effects can lead to a speedy, lessening of stress and provide feelings of calmness and good well-being of the entire body. Cannabis oil can help in getting a sound night's sleep/rest, which is known to reduce anxiety and stress.
Cannabinoids, which are in the oil, are the ones who create a positive emotional response in the nervous system of our body as it helps to relax the entire system and prepare the body for work later on.

Appetite and Obesity
Cannabis oil has been found to be very useful in stimulating hormones in our body, which will be in time to be a good, reliable helper for appetite reduction and preventing obesity. On the opposite, it can also help stimulate appetite and may help in treating anorexia. It's just a matter of adequately manipulating the cannabinoids in the cannabis oil being used or made. Therefore, those who wish to reduce weight can take refuge in cannabis oil to achieve a quick result. If you have been looking for an appetite booster, look no more.

Asthma
Cannabis has been traditionally used for the treatment of asthma and other respiratory problems. With such capabilities, cannabis oil may be an effective natural treatment for asthmatic patients because of its ability to lessen the inflammation of bronchial tubes, which are a pathway for in the inflow of oxygen into the respiratory system. It has been found to improve the symptoms of Asthma and hence could be used in its treatment and cure. Also, early reports have revealed the presence of an active ingredient in cannabis essential oil that can prevent the effects of Asthma.

Heart Health
Cannabis oil contains active properties that are considered antioxidants that have been proven to be very beneficial for the total wellbeing and functioning of the heart. Further studies show how using cannabis oil as part of treatment can help prevent cardiovascular diseases, most of which include: heart attacks, atherosclerosis, catarrh, and strokes.
This study also reveals that those who regularly consume cannabis oil have a reduced chance of having a stroke. The increasing number of strokes is drawing a global concern, so anything that can prevent it especially important to know.

Pain Relief
One of the essential historical applications of the cannabis plant oil has been to help lessen pains and inflammation and pain in the body. Cannabis oil has a great ability to cure chronic pain as well as inflammation, which is why a lot of cancer patients use it while doing chemotherapy, and medical experts have highly recommended it.

Cancer

It has been discovered by scientists that the various cannabinoids in the marijuana plant bring a lot of positive and beneficial effect in cancer treatment

It has been pointed out in this paragraph, the combination of cannabis oil and other chemotherapy has proven to be useful in treating cancer. This is one of the recent improvements in the medical world as so many people have cancer, and any treatment of this is a quantum leap. Another treatment of cancer, which is gaining more attention in the health industry, is the use of nanotechnology, though for now, it is still the product of laboratory investigation. Treating with cannabis oil remains the safest for now since it has no side effect, and it has proven to be successful.

The recommended dosage for cancer treatment per day would take three doses and after which can be increased by a gram per day. This may take about ninety days if the one using is good in following the routine. Specific guides have already been released on how to apply is most especially on states that have legalized marijuana for medical use.

Skin Protection

Cannabis or marijuana oil can be used topically to maintain glowing and healthy skin. If used on the skin, it will promote new cell growth while shedding skin cells that are dead. It can also do exfoliation of the skin and promote the growth of new skin cells to replace the older ones. Using cannabis oil as you use an after-sun gel will help the skin feel relaxed, calm, and comfortable, and it also helps in making it smooth. It can also be utilized as a topical treatment for skin irritations brought by eczema, psoriasis, and atopic dermatitis and itching.

One of the most potent uses of cannabis is in the protection of the skin. To achieve this, cannabis oil can be consumed or applied externally on the skin as it has been most effective. This is the reason while the global demand for cannabis oil is growing astronomically because of the need to maintain the skin color and beauty.

Eye Health
There are available pieces of evidence that demonstrate the ability and usefulness of cannabis oil to treat some eye conditions like macular degeneration and glaucoma, which are common among many people. Glaucoma is a severe disease of the optic nerve, which may cause loss of good vision and even total blindness when not properly managed or treated.

Chapter 3. : What Are Thc And Cbd?

What exactly is THC?

The main psychoactive ingredient present in the marijuana plant is referred to as THC. This is the agent that is primarily responsible for creating the feeling of being "high" that is associated with the use of marijuana. This compound works by replicating the effects of anandamide. Anandamide is a neurotransmitter that is produced naturally in the human body, and it helps in making sleeping and eating habits modulated and also to alleviate pain as perceived by our minds.

The main effects of THC include feelings of relaxation, altered senses (smell, sight, and hearing), fatigue, hunger, and reduced aggression.

The medical applications of THC

Research conducted for understanding the medicinal uses of THC shows that it might be useful in:

- Reducing the various side effects of chemotherapy, like nausea and vomiting, along with improving appetite

- Helping treat multiple sclerosis by easing painful spasms while improving bladder function
- Helping to relieve pressure in the eyes of people with glaucoma
- Alleviating specific symptoms of AIDS by increasing appetite
- They are reducing tremors experienced in cases of spinal injury.

What is CBD?

The chemical formulas of THC and CBD are the same. However, the atoms are arranged differently in CBD. This slight variation is what enables THC to create a psychoactive effect, whereas CBD doesn't do this. About 40 percent of cannabis extract is constituted of CBD. There is plenty of it that's available in nature, and this, coupled with the fact that it doesn't make the user "high," makes it a right candidate for medical use.

The main effects of CBD include the reduction of psychotic symptoms, reduction in levels of anxiety, reduction in inflammation, and relief from convulsions as well as nausea.

The medical applications of CBD

Research shows that CBD can be quite helpful in reducing the psychotic symptoms caused due to schizophrenia and helps manage social anxiety disorder by reducing the levels of anxiety. It can be successfully used for treating depression by decreasing depressive symptoms in an individual. It can also be used for managing the side effects of cancer treatments by stimulating appetite and reducing pain and nausea.

How to Obtain and Use Cannabis

Individuals who use cannabis oil as a means of treating different health conditions ingest it into their body with an oral syringe or by adding it to a fluid that masks its potency. The dose measurement and frequency are mainly based on the health condition being treated and the patient's cannabis tolerance level; this level can be ascertained through a doctor or health expert. Most patients often start with a small amount and then increase the treatment doses over a long period depending on their cannabis tolerance level. You need to know your level of tolerance to avoid abusing this drug.

It's difficult, if not impossible, to buy cannabis oil online or at a local pharmaceutical store, the reason is not far-fetched as there are vast regulations on the sales of the oil. Some states provide individuals with cannabis strictly for medical conditions, and this may require a medical note or proof of injury and illness from a hospital to qualify to access this drug. Also, to obtain it, you can join a collective health group, which is a group of patients who grow and share medical cannabis with a legal right to do so. If you are going to use cannabis or marijuana oil, be sure that you got it from a reputable and reliable company that operates legally and would only offer lab-tested and pure oils

Fake cannabis oils online

There are many phony cannabis oils online, and most of them are imported and sold to patients who are in dire need of this oil. This is why it is good to read books and ask questions before paying for any cannabis oil.
Some of the cannabis, which is seen online, is degraded and wrongly produced and should not be used in treating any health problem. Medical experts recommend that you go through the legal and safe means of obtaining cannabis oil to ensure its health benefits and avoid any possible side effects. As a word of caution, please never use cannabis products, oils, or any forms if you are a pregnant woman or planning to become pregnant soon.
Studies showed shreds of evidence that pregnant women who use cannabis or marijuana products during conception will have an increased risk of the miscarriage and chances of the baby being born with defects, insufficient weight. It is not only during pregnancy where consumption of cannabis is not allowed but also when the woman is breastfeeding their child.

Chapter 4. : All About Decarboxylating

What is Decarboxylation?

If you are interested in consuming cannabis edibles, then you can either purchase the prepackaged stuff or make the edibles at home. The cannabis edibles available on the market are quite expensive and tend to have varying contents of THC. If you decide to make cannabis edibles at home, you will have absolute control over the quality of ingredients you use.

Have you ever come across any scenes in a movie where someone ends up eating raw marijuana to prevent getting caught? Their eyes tend to go wide, and a lot of dramatic gasping follows suit. Here's a spoiler alert: no such thing happens when you consume raw cannabis. Why doesn't anything as exciting as what's shown in movies happen when you eat natural cannabis? The answer to this is a process known as decarboxylation. This is essential if you want to enjoy the psychoactive effect of cannabis. Cannabinoids that are present within the trichomes present in raw cannabis flowers contain an additional carboxyl ring that's known as COOH. For instance, THCA (tetrahydrocannabinol acid) is synthesized by the plant within the trichomes present in cannabis flowers. The cannabis that's distributed through dispensaries tends to contain labels about plant materials' cannabinoid content. THCA usually accounts for a significant portion of the cannabinoid present in cannabis products that haven't been decarboxylated. THCA has different benefits, but it isn't a psychoactive ingredient, and only after decarboxylation will it be transformed into THC, the component responsible for the psychoactive benefits of cannabis.

Time and heat are the primary catalysts needed for decarboxylation. Partial decarboxylation takes place when you dry and cure cannabis for a long time. This is the reason why some marijuana can test positive for trace amounts of THC along with THCA. Smoking and vaporizing are two means through which decarboxylation instantly takes place.

The lungs can readily absorb decarboxylated cannabinoids in a vaporized form, but when it comes to edibles, the cannabinoids present take longer for our bodies to absorb. Heating the cannabinoids steadily at a low temperature allows decarboxylation to take place and activates the THC present. Once the THC is enabled, then you can easily infuse the cannabis with other ingredients to cook edibles.

Steps for Decarboxylating Cannabis at Home

Here are some simple steps that you can follow for decarboxylating cannabis at home.
Preheat the oven for 20 minutes at 225°F. Doing this helps remove any moisture from the oven.
Line an oven-safe dish with parchment paper.

Crush the buds by breaking them into smaller pieces and by getting rid of any unnecessary plant materials like seeds. Place the crushed buds on the parchment paper. Ensure that the buds aren't crowded and are evenly arranged on the paper. Place the plant material in the oven and allow it to bake at 250°F for about 25 minutes. The color of the cannabis will change from green to a shade of light brown.
Once it has reached a light brown color, bake it for another 20 minutes or so, until the cannabis is medium brown in color. Keep checking on the marijuana every 10 minutes to ensure that it isn't burning.

Remove cannabis from the parchment paper and allow it to cool for a while. The cannabis will be quite crumbly, and if you aren't careful while handling it, you will be left with powdered cannabis.
Once it has cooled down, you can roughly grind it using a mortar and pestle. I prefer using a mortar and pestle or a manual weed crusher instead of a food processor. You need coarse flakes of cannabis, almost like oregano seasoning.
Store the decarboxylated cannabis in an airtight container and keep it in a dry and dark place.
Please note that the decarboxylation process gives off a slightly pungent herbal odor, so ensure that you turn on the exhaust fan in the kitchen!

Chapter 5.   How To Extract Thc

Cannabis Oil

Cannabis is a powerful, potent medicinal herb with a great history of curing many health problems and skin infections. According to medical history accrued over the years, cannabis has been grown in many regions around the world for millennia, and its cultivation has grown with time as a result of its frequent demand and medical purpose.

Cannabis, which is also known as marijuana, points out to the liquids or oil derived from the Cannabis Sativa plant, which is typically cultivated for their highly potent trichomes and other vital usages. This seemingly sticky glue-like residue contains large amounts of a substance which is called THC, which stands for tetrahydrocannabinol, the chemical property of the plant that gives off its psychotropic and cancer-curing capacity.

Cannabis oil is found to be a strong and sticky resinous substance that is from the marijuana plant and which has found to be of great importance in the medical world. This oil has become very popular and infamous in recent years due to the movement for legalized marijuana in some countries as opposed to the laws imposed on its transportation from different parts of the world. Found to possess CBD and THC, there are a good number of health benefits that users of cannabis oil derived from it.

It is deduced from the resin of the cannabis flowers. Due to the increasing number of health issues that cannabis oil has been found to solve, it is becoming a clarion call for all to take advantage of the numerous uses of this herb. This is written so that the reader will gain useful insights on how to use cannabis oil in solving those problems that the use of chemical drugs has been unable to solve.

Cannabis is being transported to different countries and has found usefulness, though primarily misused. It has different names, according to drugs.com. Cannabis is also known by many names such as hashish, grass, ganja, marijuana, pot, weed, reefer, ganja, hemp, and so much more.

Extracting the Cannabis Oil

To extract cannabis oil from the Sativa plant, a process where a solvent is used for extraction, which yields to about three to five grams of cannabis oil per ounce of bud used. You can also use grain alcohol or alcohol, particularly isopropyl as a solvent during the extraction process, and you will then strain the rest of the concoction, which will leave cannabis oil as the residue.

This process is a rather involved and lengthy process that requires the use of some equipment to achieve. In places where marijuana is not illegal, there are a lot of places to get great quality oil that has already been extracted. It is my prediction that though the cannabis leaf is widely misused, in the long term, this oil will be a breakthrough in the medical world as enough research is currently ongoing on the usefulness of this oil. This oil is also seen to be a very good skin-nourishing oil, and one is forced to ask why this important oil with such medical uses is so strictly limited and restricted.

How to extract THC

Extraction using Alcohol
Here is described in detail the process for extracting essential oils from hemp using readily available substances and materials with minimal time. The result will be a dark, oily liquid containing more than 70% pure THC.
Materials needed:

- A jar with a wide neck and tight lid is good (glass is ideal)

- A metal jar with a handle (bigger, a coffee machine is good - "Turk")

- A bottle of 96% ethyl alcohol (the cleaner, the better)

- Any amount of hemp, from the jamb up to several glasses

- A piece of dense fabric 30 x 30 cm in size (a T-shirt is suitable)
- Eye drop bottle
- Stove (electric) and range hood

Step 1

You must carefully chop the grass and crumble the cones. Remove the seeds: we won't need the oils that they contain. Place the crushed grass in a jar and fill it with ethanol so that the small particles of grass will float on top of it. Close the jar with a lid and shake it properly. Leave the mixture for several hours, during which time shake it several more times. The alcohol must acquire a pleasant dark greenish color, with stirring, oily colored bubbles should form on its surface. Cover the metal can with a dense rag, gently pushing it in to form a cone or funnel. Pour the contents of the jar very carefully onto the cloth so that most particles of grass spill out with it. After the liquid drains, lift the rag by the edges and squeeze out the liquid that has remained.

Step 2

Now you have some green liquid which is dark in color in the metal can. To extract the remaining oil extracted from the grass, it is recommended to repeat Step No. 1. Do not throw away a good thing ... Shake the grass out of a rag into a jar and repeat Step 1. You now have twice as much dark green liquid in a metal can.

Step 3
It's a must to use an electric stove! Place a metal can on the electric stove. Then, turn one of the burners on to the smallest fire and put the jar on it. It is recommended to use an extractor hood to remove alcohol vapor. Oversee the fluid. It should boil slightly, do not increase the temperature of the burner! The goal of this step is to achieve a slight thickening of the liquid. It will take time, but patience is the key. When the liquid begins to become thicker and darker, remove the fluid away from the heat. Avoid massive thickening: it will be too hard to work with the liquid after that. If you get too thick a liquid, dilute it with a small amount of alcohol.
Cool the liquid to a temperature around 18 to 20 c or room temperature. It must have enough fluidity for transfusion into a bottle from under the eye drops. This is the desired THC extract. A small amount of alcohol in the extract is necessary to increase its fluidity. It does not affect its effectiveness.

Step 4
If you have a gas stove, do not try to boil alcohol on it! A possible explosion of alcohol vapor. To finish this step, simply place a metal can in an area where it does not bother. Alcohol will evaporate all by itself. If possible, the place should be warm and well ventilated. It will take several days.
Check the fluid density as it evaporates. If it becomes too thick, add alcohol and pour it into a drop bottle.

Chapter 6. : Complete Extraction Methods

Complete Extraction Methods

Shatter, Budder and Oil are the best-known extraction methods, but there are others such as Live Resin, Fresh Frozen, or Rosin Hash you can use. You may start with the one you prefer to get the best resin, although the elements you need will vary between them.

1. Shatter
It is known as "shatter" to an extraction with gas that at a stable temperature is solid, semi-transparent, and fragile since it breaks into pieces as glass would break. Its name means 'shatter,' which lives up to its appearance. It is a soft, solid, and crystalline substance with the appearance of orange and boiled caramel that some compare with honey when it spreads across a surface. When it is still warm, it has a consistency very similar to that product; and when it has cooled, it looks more like glass.
That solvent ends up evaporating and gives rise to the iron pressed on a paper. They say it is up to six times more potent than marijuana itself and is usually smoked in bongs or water pipes.

2. Wax or waxes

The real difference between the different types of concentrates is reduced to how the process of filtering and purification of the mixture ends, which makes the final result brittle like glass, melt like wax, or almost liquid-like oil. There are a large number of variables that affect the texture and consistency of cannabis extraction. Physical agitation, changes in temperature, and humidity can also cause a translucent oil to become an opaque wax.

This mixture of phases does not allow light to pass through it. It can acquire any texture, from lumpy to dry, through consistency of butter. In short, the cannabis concentrate is a solution of various compounds found in the plant and, as long as all the components are still in a single and homogeneous phase, the extraction will be more or less transparent.

3. Budder or BHO

If the marijuana buds are wet or damp, they should be dried well. Then, we will have to mix the product with cannabis using several meshes, so that both (butane and plant) are in contact but can be easily separated. This is achieved, for example, by placing cannabis in a mesh and introducing this kind of bag in many others, and they, in turn, in a bucket where we have previously placed the solvent, which will sneak between the grooves.

During the whole process, it is necessary to ensure that you do not inhale any of the liquid that is evaporating, as it is harmful to your health. As a result, we will see that the mixture bubbles. It will be necessary to drain the meshes to the maximum to obtain the concentrate, which solidifies taking yellow color and a sticky wax appearance that will still have to dry. It may take some time for butane to evaporate completely; therefore, it is better not to smoke nearby, since explosions could occur.

4. Oil

To make extractions of medicinal cannabis oil with a high CBD content, absolute ethanol is very effective due to its purity, because it will carry unwanted components. Examples of such unwanted components are chlorophyll (which is a good proportion of the weight of dry grass) and because it is much more manageable than, for example, butane.

However, keep in mind that ethanol is also flammable, so it is necessary to take all possible precautions. Besides, it is advisable to perform the process outside the home, outdoors. It is also necessary to obtain liquid ethanol with 99.99% purity and a 45-micron mesh, where cannabis will have to be deposited.

Usually, in any extraction, you want to take advantage of the low-quality weed we have. Still, in this case, the opposite occurs: it is intended to obtain material from plants of the highest quality. It will be achieved thanks to a fast pass through the solvent of the buds without crushing since a large concentration of cannabinoids is found on the outside of the flowers. It is important that the "washing" of plant matter is not delayed because too much chlorophyll and other components that would spoil the properties of the extract would be carried away. In this sense, it is also recommended to cool the ethanol.

After this period, the mixture is filtered (vacuum elements can be used to achieve higher purity) and spread on trays for evaporation, for which we can also use an oven at a temperature not exceeding 40 degrees. The resulting medical marijuana oil can reach more than 60% CBD. However, the results will depend on each case and the variety of marijuana used.

5. Live Resin

It is a form very similar to BHO. Still, its main difference (beyond its flavor) is that whole and frozen cannabis flowers are used. In this case, the extraction will have a very characteristic aroma that is lost during the drying process. The usual thing is to chop the marijuana, put it in containers, and put it in a cryogenic freezer or with dry ice for 12 or 24 hours at temperatures between -30 and -65 ° C.

6. Fresh frozen

The process is simple: after placing the buds in the freezer for hours, several bags are taken with a sieve to extract hashish and are placed in a bucket. The main bag is filled with water and ice and then add the vegetable and mix everything for a maximum of 10 minutes. This bag will also be placed in others with a lower sieve so that the resin is filtered. Then you have to remove the first mesh and collect the product of the following. Finally, the hashish must be dried for a few days, which will acquire the appearance of deformed churros and translucent color.

7. Rosin hash

Rosin hash is one of the cheapest ways to get hashish from the cannabis flower. It will only be necessary to get a hair straightener, parchment paper, and marijuana. It also follows a straightforward process that anyone can do at home. First, you have to heat the iron and then take the paper and put it in it a small amount of marijuana with resin. The paper must be closed in such a way that the content cannot go outside. Then, press with the iron on so that the plant components evaporate and get impregnated in it. The operation can be repeated several times until all the product is obtained, which will be picked up with metal tweezers, already solidified.

It is a relatively affordable and homemade technique, which does not require the use of dangerous products or dirties in the workspace. The tools needed for the process are very few compared to others that require special bags, liquids, buckets, filters, ovens, and another laboratory equipment. Just be careful with the hot part of the iron, so it is recommended to wear thermal gloves if necessary. Also, this technique is fascinating for those who need therapeutic cannabis to access their medicine in a clean, quality way and a matter of seconds.

8. Dry sieving extraction

It is a way of obtaining resin without using any solvent, only by force. It is necessary a mesh with a specific micrometer and vibration force, which we can obtain by using an electric rotary extractor or a traditional one that must be manually operated. In this case, it is also recommended to freeze the herb, although only a couple of hours and before putting it in the extractor to increase the amount of resin obtained. It will be the machine and the arms that will do all the work and those that will make that resin detach from the marijuana and fall into the mesh. Of course, you can also do a sieve by hand. The filter, in this case, is very important, since depending on the micraje (thickness of the mesh) it will filter more or less pure trichomes (the resinous glands that contain the highest concentration of THC, CBD, CBN, and other cannabinoids). If you use meshes of a higher micron, you will get hashish with more significant residues of vegetal matter. In the video example, a 150-micron sieve has been used. Users usually prefer to use lower buds with leaves and branches to make hashish, but keep in mind that if we use the superior buds, with a higher concentration of trichomes, we will obtain a more robust and higher quality hashish.

Chapter 7. : Guide On How To Calculate Thc Dose For Recipes

Calculating THC

One of the significant differences between edible consumption of the past and the present is dosage control. The sophisticated consumer can now create an elite foundation of oils and butter with specific THC calculations, resulting in a consumable meal without angst.

The scientific determination of THC levels is calculated with basic math and the knowledge of any cannabis product (i.e., Bud, Shake, and Trim). Knowing the present levels of THC is what makes the difference between having a tremendous edible experience and shying away in fear, as many first-time consumers do. I was one of those consumers.

Knowing how to compute THC will also be a way for you to avoid overdosing and, at the same time, in able for your body to react well to your edibles. This is the first and most important recipe in your arsenal.

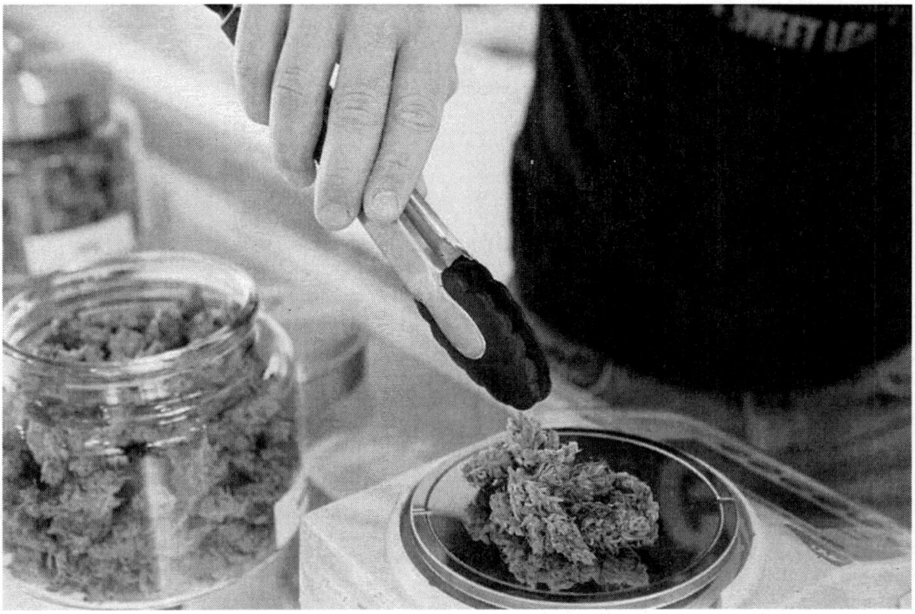

How to Calculate

*For ease of demonstrating how to use the formula I will use a THC level of 10%
1 gram of cannabis is equivalent to 1,000mg of dry weight, with a THC content of 100mg.
Newbies can start with 5-10mg of THC per serving, assuming they are going to take more than one (ex: a cookie)
Convert your cannabis from grams to milligrams.
- 28.3 grams is approximately equal to 1 ounce
- 28.3 grams x 1,000 equals 28,300 milligrams of THC.
- 28,300 x 10% (THC level) equals 2,830 mg of THC per batch.

2830 divided by 32 Tbsp. (1 pound of butter) equals 88.4 mg of THC per Tbsp. of butter.
To determine the dosage level per serving, take the total number of THC your dish has, and divide by the number of servings it yields.
At the high levels (88.4 mg THC), if your dish calls for 1 Tbsp. of butter and yields 6 servings, then your THC level per serving would be about 14 mg per serving (88.4/6).
There are also several apps and websites available online that you can also use to calculate the THC levels of your material with greater ease.
Recipes in this cookbook will also tell you how much THC content there is for the cannabis used. You are more than free to make adjustments. Like for example, if a recipe calls for 1 cup can of butter and you think it's too much for you, maybe you can substitute a third or half with regular butter.
If you don't know the THC content of your cannabis, you may also use the following infusion guide and maybe start with ¼ teaspoon to see how your body reacts to its potency.

		5%	10%	15%	20%	25%	30%
CANNABIS FLOWER USED IN INFUSION (GRAMS)	5	2.1	4.2	6.3	8.3	10.4	12.5
	7.5	3.1	6.3	9.4	12.5	15.6	18.8
	10	42.2	8.3	12.5	16.7	20.8	25
	12.5	5.2	10.4	15.6	20.8	26	31.3
	15	6.3	12.5	18.8	25	31.3	37.5
	17.5	7.3	14.6	21.9	29.2	36.5	43.8
	20	8.3	16.7	25	33.3	41.7	50
	22.5	9.4	18.8	28.1	37.5	46.9	56.3
	25	10.4	20.8	31.3	41.7	52.1	62.5

Chapter 8. : Tips And Tricks For Cooking With Cannabis

Below are my suggested tips that will help you avoid mistakes when cooking with weed.

1. Don't forget to calculate dose and power

This is considered the most crucial step that enables us to cook with cannabis correctly. Not being able to know how potent the marijuana you are using, you can't know if the concentration of cannabinoids you use in your recipes is correct and adequate. Make sure to obtain reliable information about the potency of your weed.

If you are a novice, one safe way is to start with small doses and observe how your body will react. In this case, you will avoid having an overdose.

This will change your experience with the edible, as it will allow you to get a clearer idea of the cannabinoid concentration and how to divide the doses. Once you see that your body reacts well, then you can use that dosage, or if there's no effect, let's say after an hour, add another small dose and see how your body reacts.

2. Don't put the bud directly to your food

As much as possible, never put your dried weed directly on your food as it will just give off a very unpleasant taste. The best way to cannabinoids to your recipes is to prepare cannabis oil, butter, and milk.

3. Make sure to clean your Weed

Some growers have used chemicals as their fertilizers and insecticides, and this will make your weed have impurities that will give off a horrible taste.
So, make sure to clean the herb with distilled water 3 days, then change the water every 12 hrs... Next, blanch your buds by boiling it in water for almost 5 minutes, then soaking it in an ice bath for a minute. After doing this, you can now dry and decarboxylate your weed.

4. Never Forget to Decarboxylate

Decarboxylation is a process that removes that will activate cannabinoids, which will give you its psychoactive properties. If you decarboxylate first, you will ensure that there are more cannabinoids in the food faster.

5. Crush your grass properly

The ideal way to get the right consistency of your grass is to break the weed using your hand once it is blanch and clean it. If you crush your grass too much, you will end up with tiny, sandy grass scales scattered throughout the meal. And when preparing cannabis oil or butter, you must shred the herb into pieces that are large enough to get caught in a colander or cheesecloth.

6. Do not compress too much

Almost all the cannabis butter or oil recipes we have read say that you have to squeeze the herb to separate it from the fat. You can squeeze a little, but don't overdo it.
If you compress the herb too much, you will also extract the chlorophyll from the plant, and add it to the oil/butter. This will change the taste and color of the oil or butter, and not for the better. The taste of chlorophyll is very bitter and very strong.

7. Have the proper oven temperature

This must be carefully practiced when cooking or decarboxylating your weeds because you may lose a lot of potencies if cooked above 190 ° C. However, and we tend to be safe, so we advise you to keep your oven temperature below 176 ° C. And, in case the thermometer is not very precise, keep the temperature below 170 ° C

8. Label and store edibles properly

Be sure to store and label your weed and edibles properly and keep away from arms reach of adults who must not ingest it, children, and pets.

Chapter 9. : Infusing Oils And Butter

Canna oil

Canna oil is one of the best ways to add cannabis to your meals. It is not too strong and will help you avail of all the benefits of the leaves. Most recipes that are made using cannabis plants make use of canna oil, as it is easy to incorporate. Canna oil is natural to make and can be made at home. You can also buy it online if you don't have the time for it.

Materials needed
- 1 cup decarboxylated canna leaves
- 2 cups sunflower oil
- Strainer

How to:
1. Crush the leaves lightly and add to a bowl.
2. Add in the oil and give it all a right mix.
3. Place the oil on heat and allow it to come to a boil.
4. Once it heats, simmer for 6 to 8 hours straight.
5. This will ensure that all of the flavors release into the oil.

6. Run the oil through the filter to separate the leaves from the oil.

7. Store the oil in glass bottles so that they keep fresh for longer.

8. You can use it in all your recipes.

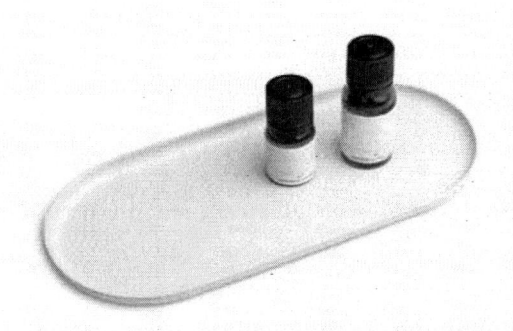

Cannabutter

Cannabutter is a lot like canna oil. You can use it in your cooking to enhance the flavor of the dish. It will be a little more potent compared to the oil, as you will use a bit of the leaf in the cooking. Cannabutter can occasionally be used to make a particular dish as it is quite potent in its THC content and will lend your dish a kick. You can consider using it for baking as the leaves will further crisp up and give the dish a unique flavor.

Materials needed:
- 1 cup decarboxylated canna leaves

- 1 cup butter

How to:
1. Allow the butter to reach room temperature and completely soften up.
2. Meanwhile, line a small baking tin with cling film and set aside.
3. You can microwave it if you like but ensure that you don't completely melt it.
4. Once it turns to a mash able consistency, you can add it to a blender along with the decarboxylated leaves and blend until well combined.
5. Once done, add it to the baking tin and use a spoon or spatula to flatten it on all sides.
6. Place it in the fridge to harden.
7. Once done, you can remove the cling film and slice the butter to be added to your dishes.

Cannabis-Infused Olive oil

Materials:
- 2 ounces marijuana, finely ground
- 7 cups virgin olive oil

How to:

1. Place a saucepan over medium heat. Add oil. When the oil is heated but not boiling, melts, add marijuana powder, and stir with a wooden spoon.
2. Lower heat and simmer. Let it remain in this state until bubbles begin to form.
3. Remove from heat. Cool thoroughly.
4. Again, place on low heat and heat until the bubbles begin to form.
5. Remove from heat and set aside for 2-3 hours.
6. Strain into a container. Squeeze the residue. Fasten the lid.

Note: You can replace olive oil with any other oil like coconut oil, canola oil, etc.

Cannamilk

Materials needed:
- 1 liter of full-fat milk or whole cream milk
- 25 grams of marijuana buds
- Heavy bottomed saucepan
- Cheesecloth
- Mixing bowl

How to:
1. In a mixing bowl, add milk and your Marijuana buds with your milk and mix them using a whisk

2. Next, heat a pot to a medium light until boils.

3. Decrease the boiling water to low heat and place the bowl, so that the bottom of the pan touches the hot water inside the container.

4. Slow cook on little light the Milk, while stirring from time to time.

5. Allow the Cannamilk to cook for 30 minutes or even longer, maybe 3 hrs. Which will depend on how strong or potent you want it to be.

6. After which, strain milk and cannabis buds using a cheesecloth to eliminate extra buds and leaves, and store in the chiller.

Canna tea

Canna tea, also known as marijuana tea, is quite a unique way to incorporate weed in your diet. Canna tea is extensively consumed in Asian and African countries to avail of its medicinal benefits. As mentioned earlier, you can improve your overall health by consuming cannabis, and one great way to do so is by chugging the tea regularly.

Materials:
- 1 cup of water
- 1 teaspoon cannabutter
- 1 tea bag

How to:
1. Add the cannabutter to a cup and mash it down.

2. Add in the teabag to it.
3. Add in the boiling water and stir it.
4. Allow the butter to dissolve into the water completely.
5. Remove the tea bag and consume the tea.
6. You can add milk to a cup and add it to the tea. You can add in any sweetener you like including sugar and honey. This brew can be used in your recipes, including sweets and savories.

Cannabis Tincture

Materials:
- 2-quart glass jar, sanitized
- Vodka or high proof alcohol like Everclear as required
- Mint sprigs as required
- Marijuana as required, finely powdered to fill the jar up to ¾

How to:
1. Add mint sprigs to the glass jar.
2. Add marijuana to fill up to 3/4 the jar.

3. Pour alcohol to fill up the jar (up to an inch above the 3/4 level).

4. Fasten the lid and place it in a cool, dark place. Shake the jar a couple of times a day. Repeat this process for 2 - 3 days.

5. Strain with a cheesecloth or a fine wire mesh strainer into a liquid dropper bottle.

6. Use as directed by your doctor.

Chapter 10. : Appetizer Recipes

1. Weed Crab Stuffed Mushrooms

Preparation Time: 10 mins
Cooking Time: 20-25 mins
Servings: 8-10
Ingredients:
24 pcs fresh whole mushrooms. Portobello is ideal (Small to medium size)
2 tbsp. cannabutter
1 tsp lemon juice
3 tbsp. Melted cannabutter. For brushing pan
¾ cup pepper jack cheese, grated
1 green onion stalk, finely minced
1 cup crab meat, cooked and diced
½ cup breadcrumbs
1 egg, beaten
½ teaspoon dill weed
¼ cup white wine
Few basil leaves, cut into thin strips
Directions:
Preheat oven at 350F. Brush 3 tbsp. Melted butter into a pan. Remove mushrooms stem and clean the caps inside. Chop up the remaining stems. Then, heat 2 tbsp. of butter in a saucepan over medium heat until melted. Add the onion and mushroom and cook for about 3 minutes. Once cooked, remove from heat and stir in lemon juice, crab meat, breadcrumbs, egg, dill, and ¼ cup pepper jack cheese.

Place mushroom caps into the baking pan and coat them with the butter. Arrange the mushroom, cavity side up, and stuff with the crab mixture. Top with the remaining cheese and pour wine into the pan (but not on top of mushrooms) Bake for 15-25 minutes or until cheese is melted and slightly browned. Top with sliced basil to finish.

Nutrition:
Calories: 186
Fat: 9.6g
Fiber: 4.2g
Carbs: 18.4g
Protein: 9.3g
THC Content: 22.5mg

2. Mary Jane's Artichoke Dip

Preparation Time: 10 minutes
Cooking Time: 30 minutes
Servings: 8
Ingredients:
3 tbsp. mayonnaise
240g roasted bell peppers
2 tbsp. cannabutter
500g marinated artichoke hearts
1 stalk green onion, diced
¾ cup parmesan cheese, shredded
Directions:
Preheat oven at 350F, Drain and chop roasted bell pepper and artichoke hearts. Melt cannabutter over medium heat and add sliced leeks. Cook until leeks are tender. Put artichoke hearts, peppers, parmesan, and mayo into the pan. Mix well then transfer to an oven-safe baking dish. Bake for about 30 minutes or until lightly browned and bubbly. Serve with flatbread or tortilla chips.
Nutrition:

Calories: 228
Fat: 12g
Fiber: 4.7g
Carbs: 27.9 g
Protein: 4g
THC Content: 23.6 mg

3. Booboo Bama's Black Beans Hummus

Preparation Time: 10 mins
Cooking Time: 0 mins
Servings: 8-10
Ingredients:
1 clove garlic
1 ½ tbsp. tahini
¼ cup cannaoil
15 oz. black beans in a can, drain and set aside liquid
2 tbsps. Lemon juice
¾ tsp cumin
¼ tsp cayenne pepper
Directions:
Put all ingredients into a blender or food processor and blend until smooth. Adjust the taste and serve with Greek olives, pita chips, or bread.
Nutrition:
Calories: 150
Fat: 8.6g
Fiber: 5.2g
Carbs: 14.4g
Protein: 5.5g
THC Content: 33.6 mg

4. Flying High Chicken Wings

Preparation Time: 15 mins
Cooking Time: 45 mins to 1 hr.
Servings: 12
Ingredients:
25 chicken wings
1/2 cup of cannabutter, melted
6 ounces of tomato sauce, canned will work
1/2 cup of red-hot sauce like Tabasco
1 teaspoon of chili powder
1 teaspoon of garlic powder

Directions:
Preheat your oven to 400 degrees F. Place plain wings in the oven and bake them for 25 minutes, or until cooked through/to your liking. Next, melt your cannabutter in the microwave and combine it with the hot sauce, the tomato sauce, the garlic, and chili powder in your large bowl. Mix and toss the cooked wings in the sauce mixture a few times, making sure to coat them relatively thoroughly and covering each wing with about the same amount of sauce. Return the coated wings to your baking sheet. Reduce oven to 250 and bake for another 20 minutes. Next, take them out of the oven. Let them cool for about 5 minutes and serve.

Nutrition:
Calories: 404
Fat: 30g
Fiber: 0.7g
Carbs: 12.4g
Protein: 20.7g
THC Content: 49.5

5. Canna Sweet Potato Fries

Preparation Time: 10 mins
Cooking Time: 20-30 minutes
Servings: 2-4
Ingredients:
1 lb. orange sweet potatoes, peeled if desired
Sea salt to taste
1 small clove garlic, finely minced
1 tablespoon cannaoil
1 tablespoon flat-leaf parsley, chopped
2 tablespoons parmesan cheese, grated
Directions:
Preheat oven to 450°F. Rinse the sweet potato pieces and dry by patting with kitchen or paper towels. Cut the sweet potatoes into fries. Spread the sweet potatoes on a baking sheet. Sprinkle salt and oil all over them. Toss well. Spread evenly all over the baking sheet without overlapping. Bake for 20 to 30 minutes. Meanwhile, add garlic, parsley, and cheese into a bowl and stir. When the fries are ready, transfer to the bowl of cheese and toss well.
Serve right away.
Nutrition:
Calories: 128
Fat: 3.5g
Fiber: 3.4g
Carbs: 22.9g
Protein: 1.8g
THC Content: 29.5 mg

6. Cannabis Deviled Eggs

Preparation Time: 35 mins
Cooking Time: 15 mins
Servings: 6
Ingredients:
6 large eggs, hardboiled, peeled and halved
2 tablespoons mayonnaise
1 tablespoon cannabutter, melted and cooled
1 to 2 tablespoons sweet pickle relish
1 teaspoon finely minced shallot
1 teaspoon Dijon mustard
Salt
Coarsely ground black pepper
Smoked paprika, for dusting
Directions:
Place the eggs on your work surface. Gently remove the yolks and place them in a medium bowl. Set the whites aside on a large plate. To the bowl, add the mayonnaise, canna-butter, relish, shallot, and mustard and mash everything together until smooth. Season with salt and pepper. Carefully fill the cavities of the egg whites with the yolk mixture. Sprinkle with the paprika.

Once stuffed, you have a day, maybe two to consume them. If you must, cover them with plastic wrap as tightly as possible and refrigerate. If you have a bunch, sandwich them together and wrap well. You can also mash the stuffed eggs and make a rad deviled egg salad sandwich. Add lettuce and tomato and spread the bread with a little Dijon mustard.

Nutrition:
Calories: 111
Fat: 8g
Fiber: 0.2g
Carbs: 3.1g
Protein: 7.1g

THC Content: 31.5g

7. Weed Potato Balls

Preparation Time: 20 mins
Cooking Time: 15 mins
Servings: 4-6
Ingredients:
Egg yolks from 2 large eggs
4 large whole eggs
500 grams of mashed potato
60 grams of green onions, finely chopped
15 grams of all-purpose flour
125 grams of cheddar cheese, grated
2 tbsps. Cannabutter
400 grams of breadcrumbs
500 ml of vegetable oil
Directions:
Take the two egg yolks, mashed potatoes, cheese, onions, and the flour and mix it all in a bowl.
Roll the mixture into small croquette sized balls as per your preference of size and refrigerate for two hours. To create the batter, whisk the 4 eggs in a bowl and keep the breadcrumbs in a separate bowl. Place a pan over medium heat and mix the vegetable oil and the cannabutter. Wait till the oil begins to bubble with the temperature. Remove the balls from the fridge and bind them in the batter by rolling them in the eggs first and then in the breadcrumbs. Fry the croquettes in the cannabis-infused vegetable oil for around 4-5 minutes until the croquettes are a golden brown and deep-fried.
Remove excess oil by rubbing on rice or bread that you can consume later. Enjoy!
Nutrition:
Calories: 257
Fat: 12g
Fiber: 1.8g
Carbs: 14.9g

Protein:
THC Content: 40.1 mg

8. Cannabis Calamari

Preparation Time: 20 mins
Cooking Time: 15 mins
Servings: 4
Ingredients:
1 whole organic egg
60 ml of cannabis milk
200 grams of dry breadcrumbs
Black pepper
Salt
500 grams of fresh calamari rings
125 grams of all-purpose flour
950 ml of vegetable oil
Directions:
The first step is to create the batter by whisking the egg with the cannabis milk in a large bowl. Add in salt and pepper to taste, and the breadcrumbs in a separate, shallow bowl.
Take the calamari and gently cover it with the flour. Shake off all the excess flour to ensure the excellent frying ability. Once done, sink it into the canna milk mixture to bind the flour and proceed to roll it in the bread crumb mixture. Refrigerate all the battered calamari rings for around 20 minutes. Take a deep fryer and pour in the vegetable oil. Allow the oil to boil and keep placing in calamari rings in batches – each batch should be fried for approximately 3 minutes until they turn a light golden! Repeat the process until all the rings are cooked.
Nutrition:
Calories: 290
Fat: 17.9g
Fiber: 2.9g
Carbs: 34.9g

Protein:
THC Content: 39.1 mg

9. Chicken Caesar Salad

Preparation Time: 20 mins
Cooking Time: 30-40 mins
Servings: 2-4

Ingredients:
2 grams of ground cannabis or 2 tablespoons of cannabis oil
2 large chicken breasts
250 grams of Romaine lettuce
2 large tomatoes
One chopped cucumber
Half a cup of breadcrumbs (dried)
Quarter a cup of store-bought Caesar salad dressing
A quarter of a cup of cheese of choice
4 tablespoons of bacon bits
2 tablespoons of olive oil
Salt and pepper
Italian herbs

Directions:
NOTE: In case you wish to use canna oil rather than go through the cannabis baking process, you can add the canna oil into the salad dressing. Pour salad dressing into a bowl and mix the canna oil into it. Using this canna oil over your salad would help you reap the benefits you require!
Take the ground up cannabis and distribute it consistently over a flat cookie baking sheet lined with parchment paper. Preheat the oven to 330 degrees Fahrenheit and bake the bud grind for around 40 minutes. Open the oven and toss occasionally to avoid burning.
Remove the dried herbs and keep it aside.

While cannabis is baking, fry the chicken in olive oil on a pan. The chicken will be fried when it is brown on both sides, and you can check tenderness with a knife and fork. It should take approximately 10-12 minutes to fry. Add salt and pepper and Italian herbs while frying for added taste. Shred the lettuce into smaller sizes. Infuse lettuce with either canna oil-infused dressing or sprinkle consistently with the ground up baked cannabis and use a spatula to distribute evenly over the leaves.

Drizzle the salad leaves with the Caesar salad dressing if not done already. Add the cheese, bacon bits, shredded and fried chicken breast, tomatoes, cucumber, salt, and pepper to taste.

Nutrition:
Calories: 2493
Fat: 36.3g
Fiber: 3.3g
Carbs: 30g
Protein: 30.3g
THC Content: 51.6 mg

Chapter 11. : Savory Meals

10. Smokin' Mac & Cheese

Preparation Time: 20 mins
Cooking Time: 30-40 mins
Servings: 12-14
Ingredients:
½ Cup of cold cannabutter plus one tablespoon of melted cannabutter
½ Unsalted butter
1 Cup of Flour
4 Cups of milk
2 Teaspoons of salt
¼ Teaspoon of cayenne pepper
1 A teaspoon of black pepper
1 A pound of penne pasta
1 Cup of shredded smoked mozzarella
1 Cup of shredded cheddar cheese
1 Cup of shredded American or Swiss cheese
¾ Cup of grated parmesan cheese
¼ Cup of breadcrumbs

Directions:
Heat your oven to 350 degrees to get going. Mix and melt both; the cannabutter and regular butter over medium heat in a large pot. After they are melted, whisk in the flour and keep whisking and mixing until cooked, usually around 4 to 5 minutes. In a separate medium-sized pot, boil the milk over high temperature. After boiling it, add the hot milk to the butter and flour mixture, whisking in to ensure that they are appropriately mixed. Add in some salt, black pepper, and cayenne pepper, then continue to cook until the entire mixture is boiling.

After it has reached the boiling level, eliminate from the heat and stir in the already cooked penne pasta and all the cheeses, and around a ¼ cup of Parmesan cheese to sprinkle on the top of it. Dispense the pasta mixture into a greased baking plate, and mix the breadcrumbs with the remaining cheese, and add in 1 tablespoon of melted cannabutter to the mix.

Shake the blend on the top of the pasta and bake it for 30 to 40 minutes until it gets golden brown. Serve and enjoy!

Nutrition:
Calories: 289
Fat: 13.8g
Fiber: 0.4g
Carbs: 30g
Protein: 11.3g
THC Content: 51.6 mg

11. Chong's Mini Burgers

Preparation Time: 15 mins
Cooking Time: 20-5 mins
Servings: 3-4
Ingredients:

3 small brown onions
250g of beef mince
1/3 cup of dried breadcrumbs
One lightly beaten egg
1/2 cup of tomato chutney
20g of cannabutter
Two tablespoons of brown sugar
One tablespoon of balsamic vinegar
Canna-Oil, for coating
Six hamburger buns
Cheese Slices
Sliced Tomatoes and Onion

Directions:

Start to chop about half an onion finely. Put the following into a bowl; chopped onion, mince, breadcrumbs, egg, and one tablespoon of chutney. Next, season with salt and pepper and start to mix them. After everything is mixed, roll a tablespoon into the mixture to make a big ball as possible. Squash them slightly to get a hamburger shape and put them in the fridge for about 10 minutes on a platter. Next, you must spray a large frying pot with your Canna-Oil. Warmth over medium-high heat. Cook 6 patties for 3 to 4 minutes each side or till it is cooked through. Ensure you don't overcook them. Medium well is the greatest for this formula, by the way. If you need a slightly higher dose of THC, you could likewise pour a teaspoon of your Canna-Oil into your combination before you start to fry it. Finally, cut your buns and put the mini burgers inside them. Tribute with a cheese slice and tomatoes. Serve and enjoy!

Nutrition:
Calories: 453
Fat: 13.9g
Fiber: 1.5g
Carbs: 51g
Protein: 29.7g
THC Content: 35mg

12. Homemade Grass balls simmered in Tomato Sauce

Preparation Time: 30 mins
Cooking Time: 40-45 mins
Servings: 10-12
Ingredients:
1 pound of lean ground beef
1 cup of fresh breadcrumbs
One tablespoon of dried parsley
One tablespoon of grated Parmesan cheese
1/4 teaspoon of ground black pepper
- 1/8 teaspoon of garlic powder
- One egg

Sauce Ingredients:
3/4 cup of chopped onion
Five cloves of minced garlic
1/4 cup of cannaoil
2 cans of whole peeled tomatoes
Two teaspoons of salt
One teaspoon of white sugar
One bay leaf
One can of tomato paste
3/4 teaspoon of dried basil

Directions:
In a large dish, mix all of the ingredients mentioned above. Mix them well and roll into small balls. Store them in a cool area until desired. In a big pot over medium temperature, add onion and garlic in the olive oil and start cooking till the onion is starting glowing. Next, stir in tomatoes, sugar, salt, and bay leaf. Conceal and decrease the heat to low temperature and simmer for 1 and a half an hour. Finally, stir in the tomato paste, the basil, 1/2 teaspoon of pepper, and meatballs and simmer for about 45 more minutes. Serve and enjoy!

Nutrition:
Calories: 257
Fat: 12g
Fiber: 1.8g
Carbs: 14.9g
Protein: 21.5g
THC Content: 51.7mg

13. Cheech's Chicken Fajitas

Preparation Time: 15 mins
Cooking Time: 20-25 mins
Servings: 8-10
Ingredients:
⅓ Cup of cannaoil
Three chicken breasts boneless & skinless •
One sliced onion
Two caps of lime juice
Two bell peppers - sliced
One teaspoon of chili powder
One teaspoon of paprika powder
Salt & black pepper
Directions:
Begin by pouring your ⅓ cup of canna Oil into a medium to large cast iron pan and place the oil on a low to medium heat so it can gradually warm up. After it is warm enough, throw your onions and bell peppers onto the pan and allow them to sauté slightly. After your veggies are sautéed, place the chicken breast onto the hot pan and allow this to steam cook. Make sure to flip over the meat with a spatula a few times to get an even coating of the cannaoil on the chicken. Top off the meat with seasonings; dust the chicken with paprika, chili powder, lime juice, salt, and pepper to create some good taste. Serve and enjoy!
Nutrition:
Calories: 287

Fat: 15.1g
Fiber: 1.6g
Carbs: 20.1g
Protein: 9.7g
THC Content: 48mg

14. Jane's Vegetarian Lasagna

Preparation Time: 20 mins
Cooking Time: 1 hr. and 15 mins
Servings: 10-12
Ingredients:
1/3 cup cannaoil
Five tablespoons of flour
About a quarter gallon of milk
Nutmeg, salt, pepper, and grated garlic
Two boxes of lasagna noodles
One huge carrot
One big red pepper
Four tomatoes
A can of olives
About 1.5 pounds of mixed cheese (mozzarella, parmesan, Gouda)
About 1.5 pounds of Portobello mushrooms
Directions:
Béchamel sauce:

Take a heavy-bottomed saucepan and pour the cannaoil into it. Heat the pan but don't allow the oil to boil. Slowly put the flour into the pot and stir energetically. Remain stirring till the flour gets golden in color. Next, gradually pour in the milk and stir without stopping till the blend begins boiling. Add salt and pepper and two teaspoons of nutmeg and keep stirring. Boil the sauce for about 5 to 7 minutes while stirring it carefully. The béchamel sauce shouldn't have any lumps, thus retain stirring until the combination is standardized. Finally, all the components are prepared, so you can start cooking the lasagna.

Lasagna:

First, cut the Portobello mushrooms into small bits, place them in a frying pot, and turn the heat up, while you add some salt. Next, fry the mushrooms till all water evaporates and 5 minutes afterward, start stirring the mixture. Switch off the heat and leave the mushrooms on a hot frying pot, allowing them to dry out even more. Though the mushrooms are resting, grate the carrot into large pieces and cut the red pepper into cubes or slices. Place the mushrooms on a plate to free up the frying pan

Use the high heat, red pepper, fry carrots, black pepper, grated garlic, and additional herbs in olive oil for about 5 to 10 seconds. Next, enhance with a little water, half a teaspoon of salt, and steam the ingredients for an additional 5 to 7 minutes without covering the pan. In the meantime, you could slice the tomatoes and olives and grate all the cheeses distinctly. Take a deep baking bowl and grease it with olive oil. Using a pass attempt brush or spoon, smear the Béchamel sauce over the whole dish space. Conceal the bottom with lasagna noodles. Shelter the noodles with 2/3 of the steamed vegetables. Pour béchamel sauce on top of it. Place the parmesan cheese consistently on top of the sauce. Place the lasagna noodles on top of the cheese. Place 2/3 of the mushrooms on top of the noodles.

Next, sprinkle the mushrooms with the rest of the parmesan cheese. Shelter the cheese with more lasagna noodles. Pour in the béchamel sauce. Shelter the sauce with the olives and the rest of the mushrooms. Cover the olives with half Gouda cheese. Put the lasagna noodles on top. Pour sufficiently the béchamel sauce and the mozzarella cheese.

Shelter this layer with more lasagna noodles and pour in some more béchamel sauce. Place the tomatoes on the top and add the rest of the vegetables and sprinkle more cheese on the top. Finally, heat the oven to 375 Fahrenheit and bake the lasagna for roughly 1 hour long.

Serve and enjoy!

Nutrition:
Calories: 345
Fat: 12.1g
Fiber: 2.5g
Carbs: 15.6g
Protein: 10.4g
THC Content: 43.6

15. Wake and Bake Breakfast Burritos

Preparation Time: 5 mins
Cooking Time: 10 mins
Servings: 2-4
Ingredients:
4 eggs
2 tbsp. cannabutter
6 oz. bacon
16-ounce refried beans
4 flour tortillas
3 ounces shredded cheddar cheese
Directions:

Cook bacon in a skillet over medium heat until crispy. Drain oil and set aside. Wrap the tortillas in foil and warm in the oven. Meanwhile, melt cannabutter in a pan and cook eggs scrambled. Heat refried beans in the same. To assemble, top each tortilla with refried beans, 2 strips bacon, egg, and cheese. Roll into burritos and serve with salsa on the side.

Nutrition:
Calories: 329
Fat: 12.1g
Fiber: 1.0g
Carbs: 29.4g
Protein: 4.6g
THC Content: 42.1 mg

16. Canna Chicken Pot Pie

Preparation Time:
Cooking Time:
Servings:
Ingredients: 12-14
1 lb. chicken breast, cooked, skinless and cut into cubes
1 3/4 cup chicken stock
1 cup green peas
1 cup diced carrots
1/2 cup diced celery
2/3 cup 2% milk
1/3 cup cannabutter
1/3 cup diced onion
1/3 cup flour
1/2 tsp salt
1/4 tsp. Crushed black pepper
1/4 tsp. celery seeds
2 9-inch unbaked pie crust

Directions:
First, preheat your oven to 385 F In a pan, combine the chicken pieces, peas, carrots, and celery and add 1/3 cup water, cover and boil for 15 minutes over medium-high heat. After that, remove it from the heat and place in a strainer to drain. Now, in the same pan, cook the onions in butter until they are soft and begin to become clear. Now, stir in the pepper, salt flour, and celery seed, subsequently stirring in the chicken broth and milk. Simmer this over medium-low heat until the mixture begins to thicken (about 10 - 15 minutes). Next, place the pieces of diced chicken in the pie crusts on separate pans. Pour the heated mixture that you just made into the over the chicken pieces. Cover this mixture with the alternate top crust and seal the edges, while trimming away and discarding excess dough. Use a butter knife to cut half-dozen slits on top to allow moisture and steam to escape. Place the pies in the oven and bake for 40 - 45 minutes, or until the top is golden brown. Take out and allow to cool for 10 minutes before serving,

Nutrition:
Calories: 318
Fat: 5.6g
Fiber: 4.3g
Carbs: 26.1g
Protein: 38.9g
THC Content: 63.0 g

17. Medical Marijuana Pizza

Preparation Time: 15 mins
Cooking Time: 25-30 mins
Servings: 14
Ingredients:
3 ½ cups flour
1 teaspoon Yeast

8 fl. oz. water
1 tbsp. white sugar
2 tbsp. cannabutter
1 cup mozzarella cheese
1 cup cheddar cheese
1 can tomatoes in can
2 tsp freshly dried oregano
Any other desired toppings
5 tbsp. cannabutter, melted

Directions:
First, add the flour, yeast, and sugar in a large mixing bowl. Then add water and steadily mix it into a dough. Cover the bowl with a damp towel or cloth and set aside in a somewhat warm area for 30 minutes. Uncover, adding the salt and 2 tbsp. of melted cannabutter, and mix into a dough ball. Coat this ball in a layer of flour. On a low temperature, cook any of the toppings you want in your 5 tbsps. Of cannabutter. Set aside. Next, add the tomatoes and oregano. Allow it to simmer, occasionally stirring, until it has the consistency of a sauce. Now, roll your dough into two separates but even balls. Flatten these and spread your sauce over the dough, subsequently adding the cheese and any more toppings you want. Bake in the oven for 20-25 minutes at 375F

Nutrition:
Calories: 420
Fat: 25.8g
Fiber: 2.8g
Carbs: 38.7g
Protein: 28.5g
THC Content: 75 mg

18. Bud Broccoli Casserole

Preparation Time: 15 mins
Cooking Time: 45-60 mins
Servings: 12
Ingredients:
1/2 cup of cannabutter
Vegetable oil for greasing
Florets from 2 heads of fresh broccoli (chopped)
3 cups of cooked rice
1 pound of shredded Cheddar cheese
1 cup of chopped yellow onion
1 cup of chopped celery
3 cloves garlic, (finely chopped)
1 cup of baby portabella mushrooms, (sliced)
1/4 cup of slivered almonds
1 x 10.5-ounce can of mushroom soup
1/2 a cup of day-old bread (cut into cubes)
Directions:
Preheat your oven to 350°Farenheit. Melt your cannabutter in a skillet over medium heat, then remove and set aside. Grease a 9 x 13-inch baking pan with the vegetable oil. Combine the broccoli, rice, cheese, onion, celery, garlic, mushrooms, almonds, and mushroom soup in a bowl and pour them all into the baking pan. Soak the bread cubes in the butter, and then spread them over the entire mixture. Bake for 45 to 60 minutes, or until golden brown and bubbling. Take it out of the oven and serve.
Nutrition:
Calories: 298
Fat: 19.5g
Fiber: 3.8g
Carbs: 32g
Protein: 19.9g
THC Content: 64.3g

19. Reuben Sandwich

Preparation Time: 5 mins
Cooking Time: 10 mins
Servings: 1
Ingredients:
2 slices rye bread
1 tbsp. cannabutter
2 ounces corned beef, thinly sliced
2 ounces sauerkraut
1/3 cup mozzarella cheese, grated
Directions:
Heat skillet over medium heat. Butter bread on one side then place buttered side down in the skillet. Layer corned beef, sauerkraut, and cheese on bread. Top with remaining slice of bread. Cook until the bread is toasted in lightly browned, the sandwich is heated through, and cheese is melted. Serve immediately.
Nutrition:
Calories: 272
Fat: 20.8g
Fiber: 2.5g
Carbs: 9.5g
Protein: 12.1g
THC Content: 29.9mg

Chapter 12. : Cookies

20. Cannabis Chocolate Cookies

Preparation Time: 10 mins
Cooking Time: 15-17 mins
Servings: 8-10
Ingredients:
1/4 cup softened cannabutter
1/2 cup softened regular butter
2 cups all-purpose flour
1/2 teaspoon baking soda
1/2 tsp salt
1 cup brown sugar
1/2 cup white sugar
1 tbsp. vanilla extract
1 egg
1 egg yolk
2 cups chocolate chips
Directions:
Preheat the oven to 325F. Grease cookie sheets or line with parchment paper. In a bowl, sift together the flour, baking soda, and salt; set aside. In a medium bowl, cream together the cannabutter and regular butter, brown and white sugar until well- blended. Beat in the vanilla, egg, and egg yolk until light and creamy, mix in the sifted ingredients until just combined. Stir in the chocolate chips by hand using a wooden spoon. Drop cookie dough 1/4 cup at a time onto the prepared cookie sheets. Cookies should be about 3 inches apart. Bake for 15 to 17 minutes in the preheated oven, or until the edges are lightly toasted. Cool on baking sheets for a few minutes before transferring them to the racks to cool completely.

Nutrition:
Calories: 250
Fat: 20.1g
Fiber: 1.8g
Carbs: 25g
Protein: 2.5g
THC Content: 45 mg

21. Weed Oatmeal Cookies

Preparation Time: 15 mins
Cooking Time: 20-25 mins
Servings: 6-8
Ingredients:
1. 4 cups uncooked whole oats
2. 1 ¾ cup ripe bananas, mashed
3. ¾ cup cannaoil
4. 1/3 cup honey
5. ¾ tsp salt
6. ½ cup nuts, chopped
7. ½ cup raisins or chocolate chips

Directions:
Preheat the oven to 350OF. Mix honey and oil in a medium bowl, make sure it is blended then add in mashed bananas and salt. Add whole oats, nuts, raisins, or chocolate chips gradually, stirring in as you go. Drop a spoonful into a cookie sheet and bake for about 20 – 25 minutes. Allow to cool for about 5 minutes and transfer the baking sheet to a cooling rack. Serve warm

Nutrition:
Calories: 235
Fat: 18.9g
Fiber: 3g
Carbs: 23.6g
Protein: 1.9g
THC Content: 41.9 mg

22. MJ's Peanut Butter Cookies

Preparation Time: 10 mins
Cooking Time: 7-10 minutes
Servings: 8-10
Ingredients:
1 cup cannabutter
2½ cups all-purpose flour
2 cups white sugar
1 cup brown sugar
2 eggs
1 tsp baking soda
1 cup peanut butter
1 teaspoon baking powder
2 teaspoons vanilla extract
Directions:

Preheat oven to 365F. Place cannabutter in microwave and heat for about 35 – 50 seconds, or until melted and make sure not to boil it or scorch it. Mix melted cannabutter with 1 cup of peanut butter and add ¼ cup flour. Add 1cup sugar, eggs, baking soda, brown sugar, baking powder, and vanilla. Add remaining flour. Place the remaining 1 cup of sugar in a separate bowl. Get a spoon and mold the cookies into balls that can fit comfortably in the palm of your hand. Roll cookies in the sugar and put them in an ungreased cookie sheet. Place in the oven and bake for about 7 – 10 minutes. You can judge for you at this point if the need another minute or two, but do not overcook it much longer than that. Remove cookies from the hot sheet and transfer them to a fresh plate and allow to cool for a minute or enjoy it warm

Nutrition:
Calories: 286
Fat: 24.5g
Fiber: 2.5g
Carbs: 29.9g
Protein: 15.7g
THC Content: 47.9g

23. Canna Sugar Cookies

Preparation Time: 10 mins
Cooking Time: 8-10 mins
Servings: 8
Ingredients:
1 cup softened cannabutter
2.75 cups flour
1 egg
½ cups white sugar
1 tsp vanilla extract
1 tsp baking soda
Directions:

Preheat oven to 374F. Mix flour, baking powder, and baking soda in a mixing bowl. In another bowl, cream butter and sugar together then add in egg and vanilla extract. Mix well. Afterwards, gradually mix in dry ingredients' mixture. Then roll dough into small balls and place on an ungreased baking sheet. Put it in the oven and bake for 8-10 mins.

Nutrition:
Calories: 245
Fat: 23.5g
Fiber: 1.3g
Carbs: 28.5g
Protein: 12.5g
THC Content: 63 mg

24. Cinnamon Pecan Cookies

Preparation Time: 15 mins
Cooking Time: 20 mins
Servings: 12-14
Ingredients:
1 cup ground pecans
½ cups sifted powdered sugar
2 cups all-purpose flour
½ tsp baking powder
1 tbsp. vanilla extract
1 cup cannabutter
1 cup brown sugar
2 tsps. Cinnamon

Directions:
Mix cannabutter and sugar in a mixing bowl until creamed together then add in vanilla extract. Mix flour and baking powder and gradually add it to your mixing bowl. Add the chopped pecans wrap the dough and chill in the refrigerator.

Remove dough from the chiller and roll into small balls before gently flattening them in your hand and placing them on an ungreased baking sheet—bake for about 20 minutes at 320F or until slightly toasted and firm to touch. Remove from the oven and gently place them in a cooling rack. Mix powdered sugar and cinnamon and then dust them with the mixture. Allow the cookies to cool completely to avoid crumbling.

Nutrition:
Calories: 254
Fat: 23.7g
Fiber: 2.1g
Carbs: 27.4g
Protein: 8.4g
THC Content: 64.1mg

25. Weed Cashew Cookies

Preparation Time: 10 minutes
Cooking Time: 12-15 minutes
Servings: 8-10
Ingredients:
4 tbsps. Cannabutter
1 cup all-purpose flour
1/3 cup packed brown sugar
1/4 tsp. salt
Topping:
1/2 cup butterscotch chips
1/4 cup light corn syrup
2 tbsps. Cannabutter
1 cup salted cashew nuts
Directions:

Preheat oven to 350Fahrenheit and put sugar in a medium mixing bowl. Blend in 2 tbsps. of cannabutter until consistency resembles crumbs. Next, add the flour and salt, mixing thoroughly. Press into an ungreased baking sheet and bake for 12-15 minutes. In a separate container, melt the butterscotch, corn syrup and 2tbspss of butter. Don't let it boil, just simmer. Pour over the cookies, then add the cashews and let cool.

Nutrition:
Calories: **224**
Fat: 11.3g
Fiber: 1.4g
Carbs: 28.3g
Protein: 5.2g
THC Content: 49.9 mg

26. Marijuana White Chocolate Macadamia Cookies with Cranberries

Preparation Time: 20 mins
Cooking Time: 15-18 minutes
Servings: 12-14
Ingredients:
3 cups all-purpose flour
1 tsp baking soda
3/4 teaspoon salt
1 cup cannabutter
1 cup brown sugar
3/4 cup white sugar
2 eggs
1 tbsp. vanilla extract
1 1/2 cups dried cranberries
1 1/2 cups white chocolate chips
1 cup coarsely chopped roasted salted macadamia nuts
Directions:

Preheat oven to 350°F. Line 2 large rimmed baking sheets with parchment paper. Sift first 3 ingredients into a medium bowl. Using an electric mixer, beat butter in a large bowl until fluffy. Add both sugars and beat until blended. Beat in eggs, 1 at a time, then vanilla. Add dry ingredients and beat just until blended. Using a spatula, stir in cranberries, white chocolate chips, and nuts. Drop dough by tablespoonsfuls into the baking sheets. Bake cookies until just golden, about 18 minutes for large cookies and about 15 minutes for smaller cookies. Let it cool before taking it out of the baking sheet to avoid crumbling.

Nutrition:
Calories: 478
Fat: 27.1g
Fiber: 2g
Carbs: 54.7g
Protein: 5.5g
THC Content: 60mg

27. Cannabis Oreo Cookies

Preparation Time: 15 mins
Cooking Time: 15-20 mins
Servings: 12-14
Ingredients:
1 cup (50 regular butter/50 cannabutter)
1 cup sugar
2 tsp salt
2 eggs
2 cups all-purpose flour
1 ¼ cups dark cocoa powder
½ tsp baking soda
For Cream Filling:
½ cup cannabutter
2 cups powdered sugar

1 teaspoon vanilla extract

Directions:

Preheat oven to 325 degrees F. In a bowl, cream together 1/2 cup cannabutter with ½ cup normal butter. Mix with the white sugar and salt until light and fluffy. Beat in eggs until fully combined. Sieve together the flour, cocoa powder, and baking soda into the mix. Blend well. Add the dry ingredients to the wet ingredients and mix until combined. Turn the dough out onto your surface and press into a flat square. Wrap the dough in plastic wrap and refrigerate for 1 hour.

For Cream Filling:

To make the filling, combine ½ cup cannabutter, powdered sugar, and vanilla extract in a medium mixing bowl. Beat together until light and fluffy. Remove the dough from the fridge, and for ease of rolling out, divide the dough into 4 pieces. To roll out the dough, place a quarter of the dough between two sheets of parchment paper. Roll the dough between the two sheets of parchment to ¼-inch thickness. Using a small round cookie cutter, cut the dough into individual rounds and place on a sizeable parchment-lined baking sheet, leaving at least ½-inch between each cookie. Pack together and re-roll out any scraps to cut additional cookies. Repeat this process with each remaining ¼ of the dough – Bake in preheated oven for 15 minutes. Remove and transfer cookies to a cooling rack to cool completely. Assemble the cookies by spreading a generous scoop of the icing onto one of the cookies and sandwiching it with another. Give it a light squeeze and scrape any excess off to clear and even out the sides.

Nutrition:

Calories: 322
Fat: 17.5g
Fiber: 3.2g
Carbs: 41.2g
Protein: 4.9g
THC Content: 48.9mg

28. Ganja Gingerbread Cookies

Preparation Time: 15-20 mins
Cooking Time: 30 mins
Servings: 12-14
Ingredients:
1/4 cup cannabutter
1/4 cup regular butter
1 egg
1 cup molasses
2 1/2 cups all-purpose flour
1 1/2 teaspoons baking soda
1 teaspoon ground cumin
1 teaspoon ground ginger
1/2 teaspoon salt
Directions:
Preheat oven to 330 degrees F. Grease and flour a 9-inch baking sheet. In a large bowl, cream together with the sugar and butter. Beat in the egg and mix in the molasses. In a bowl, sift together the flour, baking soda, salt, cinnamon, ginger, and cloves. Blend into the creamed mixture. Roll into balls or use cookie-cutter, then put in greased pan. Bake for 30 minutes. Allow to cool in pan before serving.
Nutrition:
Calories: 248
Fat: 8.4g
Fiber: 0.7g
Carbs: 40.5g
Protein: 3.3g
THC Content: 35.6mg

Chapter 13. : Bars And Brownies

29. Rocky Road Canna Brownies

Preparation Time: 20 mins
Cooking Time: 20-25 mins
Servings: 8-12
Ingredients:
1/2 cup cannabutter
1/8 cup regular butter
2 ounces unsweetened cocoa powder
4 ounces of chocolate chips
3/4 cup all-purpose flour
1/2 tsp salt
1 cup white sugar
2 eggs
1 teaspoon vanilla extract
3/4 cup toasted almond slivers
1 cup miniature marshmallows
Directions:

Preheat the oven to 350F. Line an 8-inch square baking pan with aluminum foil, and grease with either butter or vegetable shortening. Melt the cannabutter, regular butter, and chocolates over low heat in a medium saucepan stirring frequently. Set aside to cool for 5 minutes. Stir together the flour and salt; set aside. Stir the sugar into the melted cannabutter until well-combined. Beat in the eggs and vanilla and continue mixing until well incorporated. Mix in the flour and salt until just incorporated. Reserve 1/2 cup of the brownie batter and spread the remainder into the prepared pan. Bake batter in the pan for about 20 minutes. While it is baking, prepare the topping by stirring together the reserved batter with the toasted almond slivers and marshmallows. After batter in the pan has baked for 20 minutes, remove from oven. Spread topping over par-baked brownies and return to oven. Bake for about 10 more minutes or until marshmallows are browned, and when a toothpick inserted in the center comes out with just a few moist crumbs clinging to it. Let cool in pan before using the foil to lift out the brownies and slice.

Nutrition:
Calories: 407
Fat: 27.9g
Fiber: 3.7g
Carbs: 39.4
Protein: 5.8g
THC Content: 51.5 mg

30. Caramel Cashew Bars

Preparation Time: 10 mins
Cooking Time: 20 mins
Servings: 20-25 minutes
Ingredients: 8
1/3 cup brown sugar
4 tablespoons butter (2 cannabutter, 2 regular)
1 cup all-purpose flour
1/4 teaspoon salt
1/2 cup butterscotch baking chips
1/4 cup light corn syrup
2 tbsps., cannabutter
1 cup chopped salted cashews
Directions:
Heat oven to 350°F. Place brown sugar in a medium bowl. Add 4 tablespoons of butter and mix with brown sugar in a blender until it resembles coarse crumbs. Add flour and salt. Mix well. Press mixture into the bottom of the ungreased 8-inch square baking pan. Bake for 11-13 minutes and let set. Melt butterscotch chips, corn syrup, and 2 tablespoons cannabutter in 2-quart saucepan over low heat, stirring occasionally. Remove from heat. Stir in cashews. Pour cashew mixture over the crust. Continue baking for 8-10 minutes or until it starts to bubble.
Set and cool completely. Cover; store refrigerated. Cut into bars.
Nutrition:
Calories: 389
Fat: 26.9g
Fiber: 3.1g
Carbs: 41.8g
Protein: 5.8g
THC Content: 34.1 mg

31. No-bake fudge

Preparation Time: 10 mins
Cooking Time: 10 mins
Servings: 8
Ingredients:
7 cups powdered sugar
1 cup cocoa powder
1 lb. cannabutter
1 teaspoon of vanilla extract
1 cup of peanut butter
Directions:
Melt the butter and peanut butter in a saucepan or double boiler and add the vanilla essence. In a large bowl, mix the powdered sugar and cocoa powder. Add the melted ingredients and mix well, press into a flat pan, and place in the fridge until firm
Nutrition:
Calories: 325
Fat: 26.9g
Fiber: 2.5g
Carbs: 28.1g
Protein: 4.1g
THC Content: 89mg

32. Potent Blondies with Chocolate Ice-cream

Preparation Time: 6 hrs.
Cooking Time: 40 mins
Servings: 8
Ingredients:
4 tablespoons cannabis butter
1 can condensed milk
1 teaspoon vanilla extract
1/2 cup cocoa powder
2 cups heavy cream
1/2 cup cannabutter
1 cup light brown sugar
1 egg
1 teaspoon vanilla extract
1 cup flour
1/2 teaspoon baking powder
1/8 teaspoon baking soda
Pinch of salt
1 cup white chocolate

Directions:
Preheat oven to 220 degrees F. In a medium bowl, mix your condensed milk, 4 tablespoons cannabis butter, vanilla, and cocoa powder; set aside. In another bowl, whip your whipping cream until stiff. Fold your chocolate mixture into your whipping cream mixture using a spatula. Freeze for at least 6 hours. In a medium bowl, mix your cannabis butter with brown sugar using an electric hand mixer. Add your egg and vanilla and mix again. Now add your flour, baking powder, baking soda, and salt; mix again. Fold in your white chocolate using a spatula. Place your mixture on a floured baking tray and bake for 40 minutes. Serve little chunks on your chocolate ice cream.

Nutrition:
Calories: 387
Fat: 28.5g
Fiber: 4.7g
Carbs: 54g
Protein: 6.4g
THC Content: 45.9mg

33. Cannabis Cookie Bars

Preparation Time: 10 mins
Cooking Time: 15 mins
Servings: 8-10
Ingredients:
1/2 cup cannabutter
1 1/2 cup graham crumbs
1-pound powdered sugar
1 1/2 cups peanut butter
1/2 cup butter, melted
12 oz. bag milk chocolate chips
Directions:
Combine Graham cracker crumbs, sugar, and peanut butter; mix well. Blend in the melted cannabutter until well-combined. Press mixture evenly into a 9 x 13-inch pan. Melt chocolate chips in the microwave or a double boiler. Spread over peanut butter mixture. Chill until just set and cut into bars.
Nutrition:
Calories: 399
Fat: 24.6g
Fiber: 2.1g
Carbs: 45.8g
Protein: 6.9g
THC Content: 51.4 mg

34. Rice Krispy Treats

Preparation Time: 5 mins
Cooking Time: 15 mins
Servings: 12
Ingredients:
1 10 oz. bag of marshmallows
6 cups Rice Krispies cereal
1 12 oz. bag of butterscotch chips
3 tbsps. Cannabutter
Directions:
On low heat, melt cannabutter in a large saucepan or pot. Add the bag of marshmallows and mix it until the butter and marshmallows are thoroughly blended. Once they are blended well, remove from the heat. Quickly, while the mixture is still hot, add the cereal and stir until it is evenly dispersed throughout the mix. New, mix in the butterscotch pieces, stirring thoroughly. Press your mixture into a greased baking pan and let chill for at least45 minutes. After this time, you may cut the solidified mixture into whatever size pieces you please.
Nutrition:
Calories: 289
Fat: 22.6g
Fiber: 1.0g
Carbs: 40.3g
Protein: 2.3g
THC Content: 41.6 mg

35. Cannabis Peanut Bars

Preparation Time: 1 ½ to 2 hrs.
Cooking Time: 15 mins
Servings: 8-12
Ingredients:
1 cup canna butter melted
2 cup confectioner's sugar
2 cup crumbled graham crackers
1.5 cups chocolate chips
1 cup peanut butter
4 tbsp. additional peanut butter
Directions:
Mix the cannabutter, sugar, graham crackers, and 1 cup of peanut butter in a mixing bowl until well; blended. Place and press down into an ungreased 9 x 13 baking pan. Next, take a double boiler to melt the chocolate chips and 4 tbsps. peanut butter. Stir every minute or two during this process, ensuring it comes out smooth and well-blended. Spread this mixture over the mixture in the baking pan, then place it in the chiller for 1.5 to 2 hours. Take out of the refrigerator and cut into squares of your preference.
Nutrition:
Calories: 348
Fat: 28.4g
Fiber: 3.5g
Carbs: 53.1g
Protein: 2g
THC Content: 67mg

36. Weed Chocolate Brownies

Preparation Time: 20 mins
Cooking Time: 20-25 mins
Servings: 20
Ingredients:
1/4 lb. Butter
1/4 lb. dark chocolate
1 cup of white sugar
4 regular eggs
1/2 cup flour
Nutmeg
Cinnamon
2 tbsp. of vanilla extract
1 ounce of finely ground cannabis bud
Directions:
Preheat oven to 350 degrees F. Melt the butter over low heat, then add the chocolate and melt that in with the already melted butter; stir regularly. As soon as the chocolate has melted entirely, add the cinnamon, nutmeg, and the white sugar; stir and simmer for a few minutes. Add the eggs, one at a time, beating them so that the yolk breaks up. Continue to stir the mixture on a low heat until it is completely smooth. Add the flour and finely ground weed to the mix. Stir it well; if it is difficult to stir, then add a small dash of milk. Pour mixture into a greased 9x13 inch pan. Bake your mixture for 20-25 minutes, sometimes a little longer is required. Then cut it into around 20 squares
Nutrition:
Calories: 315
Fat: 29g
Fiber: 2.5g
Carbs: 54.7g
Protein: 5.7g
THC Content: 35mg

Chapter 14. : Cakes

37. Cannabis Coffee Cake

Preparation Time: 15 mins
Cooking Time: 15-20 mins
Servings: 12
Ingredients:
2 ¼ cup flour
1 tsp baking soda
2/3 cup canna milk
1 cup brown sugar
½ cup white sugar
¼ cup oil
1 tbsp. cinnamon powder
1/4 tsp salt
2 eggs
1/2 cup almonds slivers or any nuts
1 ½ tablespoons cannabutter, melted
1 tsp vanilla extract
Directions:
Preheat oven to 350F. Grease and flour an 8×12-inch pan. In a medium bowl, sift together flour, baking soda, salt, and cinnamon. Set aside. In a bowl, combine eggs, canna milk, oil, sugar, and vanilla extract. Mix well. Add flour mixture and mix well. Using a wooden spoon or a very heavy whisk, add almond slivers to batter and fold. Pour into prepared 8×12-inch pan and bake for 1 hour. Check for doneness with a toothpick. Allow to cool for at least 20 minutes before serving. You may spread cannabutter on top and dust with powdered sugar.

Nutrition:
Calories: 378
Fat: 11.6g
Fiber: 4.9g
Carbs: 63.7g
Protein: 7.7g
THC Content: 59.7mg

38. Marijuana Cupcakes

Preparation Time: 10 mins
Cooking Time: 20-25 mins
Servings: 12
Ingredients:
¼ Milk and ¼ Yogurt
1 Tablespoon of hemp oil
¼ Cup of Agave
A Teaspoon of Vanilla extract
¾ Cup of all-purpose flour
¼ baking soda
Salt
1 Tablespoon of cornstarch
1 teaspoon of baking powder
¼ Teaspoon of baking powder
Frosting:
2 Tablespoons of cannabutter
A Teaspoon of vanilla extract
2 Tablespoons of strawberry jam
2 ½ Cups of sugar

Directions:
Preheat the oven to about 330 to 350 degrees. In a medium to large size bowl, whisk together the yogurt and vanilla extract. After mixing, add all the dry ingredients into the wet; and mix properly. Line a cupcake pan with liners and fill every two thirds full of the mixture, put the pan into the oven then bake it for 20 to 25 minutes. To test if it's cooked, insert a toothpick and ensure that it comes out completely clean, meaning the cakes are cooked inside. For the frosting, mix the butter and sugar on low speed, then add in the strawberry jam a spoonful at a time. Finally, add in the vanilla and put frosting in a piping bag to garnish your cakes while cooled. Serve and enjoy!

Nutrition:
Calories: 398
Fat: 12.5g
Fiber: 4.3g
Carbs: 65.4g
Protein: 5.6g
THC Content: 49.5mg

39. Blueberry Lemon Muffins

Preparation Time: 10 mins
Cooking Time: 20 mins
Servings: 12
Ingredients:
1 cup flour
1/2 cup heavy cream
1 egg
2 tablespoons cannabutter
3 tablespoons sugar
1/4 teaspoon baking soda
1/2 teaspoon baking powder
1/4 teaspoon dried lemon zest

1/4 teaspoon lemon flavoring or extract
A pinch salt
2-ounce fresh blueberries

Directions:
Place cupcake papers in the muffin molds.
Mix flour and cream. Mix well. Add egg. Mix well.
Add canna-butter, stevia, baking soda, baking powder, lemon flavoring, salt, and lemon zest. Mix well.
Add blueberries and mix well. Pour into the muffin molds (half fill it).
Bake in a preheated oven to 350 degrees F for about 20 minutes or until golden.
Cool. Serve topped with butter.

Nutrition:
Calories: 350
Fat: 12.1g
Fiber: 5.2g
Carbs: 64g
Protein: 8g
THC Content: 35mg

40. Canna Mug Cake

Preparation Time: 5 mins
Cooking Time: 1 min
Servings: 2
Ingredients:
A box of vanilla cake mix
One tablespoon of cannabutter
2 tablespoons of unsalted butter, softened
2 tablespoons of water
Two tablespoons of egg, beaten

Directions:
Grease the insides of a microwave-safe cup with butter. Mix the water, egg, cannabutter, and unsalted butter and mix well to create a thick batter in a bowl. Add in the cake mix and beat again. Continue to beat as well as you can. Add cake and batter mix to cup and microwave for 60 seconds. Serve!
Nutrition:
Calories: 298
Fat: 8.5g
Fiber: 2.4g
Carbs: 36.5g
Protein: 2g
THC Content: 18.9mg

41. Marijuana Pumpkin Muffins

Preparation Time: 10 mins
Cooking Time: 12-15 mins
Servings: 12
Ingredients:
1/2 cup canned pumpkin puree
1 egg
3/4 cup canna milk
2 tbsp. oil
2 cups cake flour
3 teaspoons Baking powder
1 teaspoon. Ground ginger
1+1/2 tsp. cinnamon
1/2 teaspoon Ground cloves
1/4 teaspoon Salt
1/2 cup brown sugar
1 cup fresh cranberries, finely chopped
1/4 cup white sugar
Directions:

Combine pumpkin, egg, milk, and oil in a bowl. Sift together flour, baking powder, ginger, cloves, and salt in another bowl. Stir in brown sugar and mix well. Gradually pour pumpkin mixture in the bowl with flour mixture then sprinkle with cranberries. Stir just until all ingredients are well mixed. Spoon mixture into 12 muffin liners on a muffin tin. Bake at 400f for 12-15 minutes, let it cool in the pan for a minute then roll in granulated sugar while warm or you may add any frosting you like

Nutrition:
Calories: 388
Fat: 13.4g
Fiber: 6.7g
Carbs: 69.9g
Protein: 11g
THC Content: 57.9mg

42. Chocolate Space Cake

Preparation Time: 15 mins
Cooking Time: 20-25 mins
Servings: 10
Ingredients:
200 g all-purpose flour
200 ml of milk
2 pcs eggs
100 grams of cocoa powder
80 grams cannabutter
180 g powdered sugar or regular white sugar
Directions:

Preheat oven to 380 degrees. Put cannabutter in the microwave on low to medium heat until it is melted. Grease and flour a cake pan or use a parchment paper then set aside. Mix canna butter, flour, sugar, eggs, milk, and cocoa powder in a bowl until the consistency is smooth and lump-free. Pour the mixture in the cake pan then place it in the oven for 21 - 25 minutes. Take the cake out of the oven and let it cool. From here, feel free to use any frosting, toppings you like for your cake.

Nutrition:
Calories: 398
Fat: 22.6g
Fiber: 2.5g
Carbs: 65g
Protein: 6.8g
THC Content: 47.9mg

43. Getting High Orange Cake

Preparation Time: 15 mins
Cooking Time: 50-55 mins
Servings: 8-12
Ingredients:
  2/3 cup cannabis-infused olive oil
3 pcs oranges
1 cup of cane sugar
3 eggs
1/2 cup buttermilk
1 3/4 cup all-purpose flour
1 1/2 teaspoon Baking powder
1/4 teaspoon baking soda
1/4 tsp. salt
Whipped cream
  Directions:

Preheat oven to 350F and then begin to use a grater to grate off the peel of two of the oranges. Put the peels into a bowl containing the sugar and mix all of it when done with the two oranges. Now, cut these two oranges in half and separate each segment and cut these segments into quarters. With the remaining segments, cut it in half and juice it into a measuring cup. Add the buttermilk or yogurt to this mixture until it is 2/3 of a cup combined. Now, while mixing in the eggs and canna olive oil into the bowl of sugar and orange rind, also add the buttermilk, orange juice mixture and mix this all together. Now, put the flour, baking powder, salt, and baking soda into a sifter and sift into this bowl. Now, add the quarter pieces of the oranges. Then butter a pan (roughly 9" X 5") and pour the mixture into it, subsequently placing it in the oven for 50 to 55 mins. After this, take the cake out of the oven, let it cool for 5 minutes, serve and enjoy.

Nutrition:
Calories: 379
Fat: 12.9g
Fiber: 11.9g
Carbs: 35.6g
Protein: 11g
THC Content: 47.6mg

44. Weed Cheesecake

Preparation Time: 25 mins + cooling time
Cooking Time: 0 mins
Servings: 12
Ingredients:
2 tbsps. Cannabutter
1 tbsp. regular butter
24 Oreo cookies, crushed
3 (250 grams) cream cheese
3/4 cup white sugar

1 tsp vanilla extract
3 eggs
Directions:
Preheat oven to 33F. Place cookies in a resealable plastic bag. Flatten bag to remove excess air, then seal bag. Finely crush cookies by rolling a rolling pin across the bag. Place in a bowl, then add butter; mix well. Press firmly on bottom of a 9-inch springform pan.

Beat cream cheese, sugar and vanilla extract in a large bowl with electric mixer on medium speed until well blended. Add eggs gradually, beating just until blended after each addition. Pour mixture over prepared crust. Bake 45 minutes or until center is almost set. Cool. Refrigerate for 3 hrs. Or overnight.

Nutrition:
Calories: 287
Fat: 12.1g
Fiber: 2.1g
Carbs: 35g
Protein: 1.2g
THC Content: 38.9mg

45. Cannabis Carrot Cake

Preparation Time: 15 mins
Cooking Time: 1 hr.
Servings: 6-8
Ingredients:
1 cup canna milk
3 eggs
1 1/2 cups sugar
2 cups all-purpose flour
2 tsps. Baking powder
2 cups grated carrots
1 cup coconut flakes
1 cup walnuts, chopped

1 can crushed pineapple
2 tsps. Vanilla extract
2 tsps. ground cinnamon
1/4 tsp salt

Directions:
Preheat oven to 350F. Grease and flour an 8×12-inch pan. In a medium bowl, sift together flour, baking soda, salt, and cinnamon. Set aside. In a bowl, combine eggs, canna milk, oil, sugar, and vanilla extract. Mix well. Add flour mixture and mix well. In a bowl, combine grated carrots, coconut flakes, walnuts, and pineapple. Using a wooden spoon or a very heavy whisk, add carrot mixture to batter and fold. Pour into prepared 8×12 inch pan and bake for 1 hour. Check for doneness with a toothpick. Allow to cool for at least 20 minutes before serving.

Nutrition:
Calories: 376
Fat: 12.1g
Fiber: 5.1g
Carbs: 45.7g
Protein: 3.8g
THC Content: 51.7 mg

Chapter 15. : Drinks

46. Cannabis-Infused Hot Cocoa

Preparation Time: 10 mins
Cooking Time: 20 mins
Servings: 2-4
Ingredients:
3 cups of non-dairy milk alternative, or standard milk
½ cup of canna milk
⅓ Cup of unsweetened cocoa powder
Eight squares of 72 to 85% dark chocolate
One teaspoon of sea salt
½ cup of brown sugar
⅓ Cup of boiling water
¾ teaspoon of vanilla extract
½ cup of half-and-half cream or non-dairy creamer
Directions:
Step 1 - Mix the cocoa powder, sugar, and salt in a small bowl. In a medium saucepan on medium temperature, add your boiling water and the squares of dark chocolate. Transfer the chocolate squares around until they melt with the hot water. Next, add in your dry ingredients: brown sugar, sea salt, and cocoa powder, and whisk them with the hot water and melted chocolate. Blend in your 3 cups of milk or non-dairy substitute, as well as your canna milk, half-and-half cream, or non-dairy creamer. Increase the heat and whisk until the mixture is steaming but not boiling yet. Remove the mixture from the heat, stir in your vanilla extract, pour your hot cocoa into a mug, and enjoy!
Nutrition:
Calories: 277
Fat: 10.3g

Fiber: 3.4g
Carbs: 40.1g
Protein: 9.3g
THC Content: 35mg

47. Tiramisu Milk Shake

Preparation Time: 5 mins
Cooking Time: 0 mins
Servings: 2
Ingredients:
5 oz. canna milk
3 scoops vanilla ice cream
2 oz. espresso or pure black coffee
1 tbsp. cream cheese
1 tsp. cocoa powder
Whipped Cream for garnish
Directions:
Put espresso in a blender together with the canna milk, cream cheese, and ice cream. Blend until it has a smooth consistency. Fill in tall glass about 1/3 full then layer some whipped cream, followed by the blended mixture and top with more whipped cream. Dust cocoa powder on top. Serve immediately.
Nutrition:
Calories: 376
Fat: 45.5g
Fiber: 2.4g
Carbs: 54.1g
Protein: 5.7g
THC Content: 23.5 mg

48. Banana-blueberry smoothies

Preparation Time: 5 mins

Cooking Time: 0 mins
Servings: 1-2
Ingredients:
1 cup canna milk
1 sliced banana
1 cup yogurt
1 cup fresh strawberries, top removed
2 cups fresh blueberries
Directions:
Put all in ingredients in a blender and blend until it has a smooth consistency. Pour in a glass and serve immediately.
Nutrition:
Calories: 207
Fat: 4.9g
Fiber: 12.1g
Carbs: 26.7g
Protein: 8.9g
THC Content: 29.1 mg

49. Canna Chocolate Milkshake

Preparation Time: 5 mins
Cooking Time: 0 mins
Servings: 1-2
Ingredients:
3 scoops chocolate ice cream
1/2 cup canna milk
2 tbsp. chocolate syrup
Directions:
Put all ingredients in a blender and blend until it has a smooth consistency. For extra chocolate flavor and presentation, line the inside of a glass with chocolate syrup, pour the milkshake in and serve immediately.
Nutrition:
Calories: 288
Fat: 12g

Fiber: 1.2g
Carbs: 39.2g
Protein: 5.8g
THC Content: 18.9mg

50. Spiced Chai Bong Milk

Preparation Time: 5 mins
Cooking Time: 15 minutes
Servings: 2-4
Ingredients: 4 cups of water
1/2 cup sugar
8 cups canna milk
2 teaspoons fresh ginger, minced
12 pods green cardamom, cracked
2-inch stick cinnamon
12 whole black peppercorns
12 whole cloves
Half and half as required
2 teaspoons oil
Directions:
Add all the ingredients except half and a half to a saucepan. Place the saucepan over medium heat. Bring to the boil. Lower heat and simmer for 15 minutes. Strain and store until use.
To serve: Fill cups up to 3/4 with the strained liquid. Fill it up with half and a half — place in a microwave and heat. Serve immediately.
Nutrition:
Calories: 362
Fat: 12.3g
Fiber: 0.2g
Carbs: 49.8g
Protein: 16.1g
THC Content: 76.9 mg

51. Hot Apple Cider Drink

Preparation Time: 10 mins
Cooking Time: 30 mins
Servings: 2-4
Ingredients:
4 cups apple cider vinegar
1/4 teaspoon ground allspice
1 stick cinnamon
1/4 teaspoon whole cloves
1 tablespoon cannabis tincture
2 tablespoons brown sugar
A pinch nutmeg
Directions:
Place allspice and cloves on a cheesecloth and fasten with a string to make a spice bag. Add all the ingredients except nutmeg to a crockpot. Cook on High for 30 minutes and on Low for 30 minutes. Alternately, add all the ingredients to a pot. Place the pot on medium heat and bring to the boil. Lower heat and simmer for an hour. When done, remove the spice bag and squeeze out the liquid into the pot. Stir well. Discard the spice bag and cinnamon stick. Serve hot garnished with nutmeg.
Nutrition:
Calories: 70
Fat: 0.1g
Fiber: 0.4g
Carbs: 7.3g
Protein: 0.1g
THC Content: 37.5 mg

Conclusion

Welcome to the end of our cookbook. In this cookbook, you were given all the information that you need so that you can start cooking with cannabis. Apart from this, you were also provided all the information that you will need to understand the benefits that cannabis offers fully. The recipes in here are all tried and tested and sure to leave you with a unique taste. But you need not limit yourself to just these and come up with recipes of your own. Once you try out the recipes, you are sure to keep up with it for a lifetime! You can make them in large batches and give away to friends and families as gifts. Armed with the information given in this cookbook, you will be able to decide about the different things you must remember while cooking with cannabis. Regardless of whether you are thinking about cooking with cannabis or are already cooking with cannabis, there are inevitable mistakes that a lot of people make. By following the simple steps and tips given, you can avoid those mistakes and start cooking with cannabis like a pro! It is vital to that you've learned the necessary skills to properly integrate microdosing and cannabis cuisine adequately into a routine that works for your purpose. It is essential to remain within the recommended doses as too much can cause you to trip extensively. Marijuana is a versatile medicine, and you can implement it in any dish of your choice if there were recipes in here that struck a particular chord, practice cooking them over and over again with different doses until you find the sweet spot! Please do wait for a one-hour minimum after consuming the allocated serving of your marijuana dish before deciding to consume more since edibles do take an hour to cook in! We looked at some of the remedies that you can implement, if such a situation comes through, and can use it to avail quick relief.

Thank you to you for choosing this cannabis cookbook and hope you had a good time reading it. The main aim of this was to educate you on the basics of marijuana and how you can use it to enhance your cooking. You can also suggest this cookbook to your friends and family so that they, too, can enjoy preparing the recipes and understand what the herb is all about. There are a lot of recipes that I gave you that is good for sharing with your family and friends, most of which you can prepare ahead of time and store for late consumption. We do hope you enjoyed with numerous recipes on how to cook with marijuana and CBD oil. Have fun with cooking and integrate yourself in a way that nourishes your body medicinally and otherwise. I want to thank you once again for purchasing this book.

Now, prepare all the needed ingredients and start cooking! Wishing you the best and happy getting high! Bon appétit!

Manufactured by Amazon.ca
Acheson, AB